INTRODUCING
ISSUES WITH
OPPOSING
VIEWPOINTS®

Euthanasia

Other books in the Introducing Issues
with Opposing Viewpoints series:

INTRODUCING
ISSUES WITH
OPPOSING
VIEWPOINTS®

Euthanasia

Paul Cockeram, *Book Editor*

Christine Nasso, *Publisher*
Elizabeth Des Chenes, *Managing Editor*

GREENHAVEN PRESS
An imprint of Thomson Gale, a part of The Thomson Corporation

THOMSON

™

GALE

Detroit • New York • San Francisco • New Haven, Conn. • Waterville, Maine • London

LIBRARY OF CONGRESS CATALOGING-IN-PUBLICATION DATA

Euthanasia / Paul Cockeram, book editor.
    p. cm. — (Introducing issues with opposing viewpoints)
  Includes bibliographical references and index.
  ISBN-13: 978-0-7377-3596-3 (hardcover : alk. paper)
  ISBN-10: 0-7377-3596-1 (hardcover : alk. paper)
  1. Euthanasia—Moral and ethical aspects—Juvenile literature. 2. Assisted suicide—Moral and ethical aspects—Juvenile literature. I. Cockeram, Paul.
  R726.E7825 2007
  179.7—dc22

                                                                        2006030398

Printed in the United States of America

Contents

Foreword

Indulging in a wide spectrum of ideas, beliefs, and perspectives is a critical cornerstone of democracy. After all, it is often debates over differences of opinion, such as whether to legalize abortion, how to treat prisoners, or when to enact the death penalty, that shape our society and drive it forward. Such diversity of thought is frequently regarded as the hallmark of a healthy and civilized culture. As the Reverend Clifford Schutjer of the First Congregational Church in Mansfield, Ohio, declared in a 2001 sermon, "Surrounding oneself with only like-minded people, restricting what we listen to or read only to what we find agreeable is irresponsible. Refusing to entertain doubts once we make up our minds is a subtle but deadly form of arrogance." With this advice in mind, Introducing Issues with Opposing Viewpoints books aim to open readers' minds to the critically divergent views that comprise our world's most important debates.

Introducing Issues with Opposing Viewpoints simplifies for students the enormous and often overwhelming mass of material now available via print and electronic media. Collected in every volume is an array of opinions that captures the essence of a particular controversy or topic. Introducing Issues with Opposing Viewpoints books embody the spirit of nineteenth-century journalist Charles A. Dana's axiom: "Fight for your opinions, but do not believe that they contain the whole truth, or the only truth." Absorbing such contrasting opinions teaches students to analyze the strength of an argument and compare it to its opposition. From this process readers can inform and strengthen their own opinions, or be exposed to new information that will change their minds. Introducing Issues with Opposing Viewpoints is a mosaic of different voices. The authors are statesmen, pundits, academics, journalists, corporations, and ordinary people who have felt compelled to share their experiences and ideas in a public forum. Their words have been collected from newspapers, journals, books, speeches, interviews, and the Internet, the fastest growing body of opinionated material in the world.

Introducing Issues with Opposing Viewpoints shares many of the well-known features of its critically acclaimed parent series, Opposing Viewpoints. The articles are presented in a pro/con format, allowing readers to absorb divergent perspectives side by side. Active reading questions preface each viewpoint, requiring the student to approach the material thoughtfully and carefully. Useful charts, graphs, and cartoons supplement each article. A thorough introduction provides readers with crucial background on an issue. An annotated bibliography points the reader toward articles, books, and Web sites that contain additional information on the topic. An appendix of organizations to contact contains a wide variety of charities, nonprofit organizations, political groups, and private enterprises that each hold a position on the issue at hand. Finally, a comprehensive index allows readers to locate content quickly and efficiently.

Introducing Issues with Opposing Viewpoints is also significantly different from Opposing Viewpoints. As the series title implies, its presentation will help introduce students to the concept of opposing viewpoints, and learn to use this material to aid in critical writing and debate. The series' four-color, accessible format makes the books attractive and inviting to readers of all levels. In addition, each viewpoint has been carefully edited to maximize a reader's understanding of the content. Short but thorough viewpoints capture the essence of an argument. A substantial, thought-provoking essay question placed at the end of each viewpoint asks the student to further investigate the issues raised in the viewpoint, compare and contrast two authors' arguments, or consider how one might go about forming an opinion on the topic at hand. Each viewpoint contains sidebars that include at-a-glance information and handy statistics. A Facts About section located in the back of the book further supplies students with relevant facts and figures.

Following in the tradition of the Opposing Viewpoints series, Greenhaven Press continues to provide readers with invaluable exposure to the controversial issues that shape our world. As John Stuart Mill once wrote: "The only way in which a human being can make some approach to knowing the whole of a subject is by hearing what can be said about it by persons of every variety of opinion and studying all modes in which it can be looked at by every character of mind. No wise man ever acquired his wisdom in any mode but this." It is to this principle that Introducing Issues with Opposing Viewpoints books are dedicated.

Introduction

"There is no evidence for a slippery slope in the Netherlands: euthanasia and assisted suicide in 1995 did not involve patients whose diseases were less severe than those involved in 1990, and there were no signs that the decision-making process had become less careful."

—Peter H. Millard, St. George's
Hospital Medical School, London

"Where will it end? If we allow the elderly or incurable to be assisted in suicide, what other groups will be given this 'right'? Will the handicapped or mentally retarded be next? Will teenagers, who are the leading age group of suicide, also have this 'right to die'?"

—John Sistare, Seminarian of Diocese of Providence

Euthanasia and physician-assisted suicide are increasingly controversial topics, both in the United States and throughout the world. The prospect of both killing people who are no longer able to stay alive by themselves and of allowing people to choose their time of death raises very serious ethical, moral, and social questions. One of the greatest concerns regarding euthanasia and physician-assisted suicide is whether opening the door to one form of death and killing will invite other, more serious forms of it. This line of reasoning is usually called "the slippery slope." The slippery slope argument claims that if one form of euthanasia is allowed—euthanizing people in a persistent vegetative state, for example—then eventually another form of euthanasia will be allowed in which perhaps old people are killed against their will. At the bottom of this slippery slope lies the potential for society to allow the killing of its less desirable people, a practice known as eugenics. Nazi Germany is an example of a society that practiced eugenics: It exterminated millions of people because Germans found them to be inferior. But does legalizing one form of euthanasia in fact put society at risk for accepting the murder of innocents? The question of whether there exists a slippery slope toward

A woman tapes her mouth to represent comatose patients who might oppose euthanasia. The idea of ending the lives of unresponsive people strikes an emotional chord in America.

immorality remains central to the issue of euthanasia and physician-assisted suicide in the United States and around the world.

Those who oppose any form of legalized euthanasia fear it will encourage the acceptance of outright selective murder. Once society accepts the murder of the brain-dead or the terminally ill, they reason, what is to stop society from accepting the murder of those who are permanently disabled or whose hospital bills are too expensive? Opponents of euthanasia worry that the Netherlands, a country that practices a variety of different forms of euthanasia, is already sliding down a slippery slope. They point to a 2001 study by the Dutch government that showed that nearly 20 percent of all cases of euthanasia were involuntary, meaning that a patient was euthanized without giving consent. This would indicate that Dutch doctors in effect took that patient's life without his or her permission. This idea is wholly frightening and threatens the very trust that patients place in their doctors. As former surgeon general C. Everett Koop has said, "We must be wary of those who are too willing to end the lives of the elderly and the ill. If we ever decide that a poor quality of life justifies ending that life, we have taken a step down a slippery slope that places all of us in danger."

Indeed, it is this aspect of euthanasia that most concerns its opponents—its application to those who are unable to communicate whether they want assistance in dying or not. For example, children born with severe birth defects cannot speak for themselves whether or not they want a chance at life or if they would prefer to be euthanized to avoid suffering. In the Netherlands, such children are allowed to be euthanized at a doctor's discretion, guided by rules known as the Groningen protocol, a set of guidelines for euthanizing newborn infants or comatose patients. According to Bob Barr, a former Republican senator from Georgia, this practice constitutes a steep slide toward a moral wrong. He warns, "Parents who don't want to contend with raising a disabled child will have their baby or young child euthanized, even if the baby has a fighting chance at a meaningful life. Likewise, family members who fear the burden of coping with a disabled or comatose loved one will seek his or her involuntary euthanasia." Concerns over where one form of euthanasia may lead are the very thing that prevents many people from approving of its use in any form.

However, there are reasons to be skeptical of the slippery slope argument. In rhetoric, the formal study of argument, the slippery slope is considered to be a logical fallacy—that is, an error in reasoning or logic. Philosophers and logicians consider the slippery slope an error because it argues that the first action, in this case legalizing euthanasia for the terminally ill, is the cause of the next action, for example, allowing the murder of the elderly. But this sequence is not necessarily so, considering that the causes of any given action are complex and depend upon all kinds of variables. Therefore, critics oppose the slippery slope argument because they see no causal relationship between allowing terminally ill patients to control their own deaths and killing elderly or disabled persons against their will.

Furthermore, the fears foretold by slippery slope arguments do not always materialize. Before abortion was legalized, for example, oppo-

Former Republican senator Bob Barr believes euthanasia constitutes a steep slide toward a moral wrong.

Oregonians demonstrate in favor of their state's physician-assisted suicide law. Oregon is the only state in America where terminally ill patients can choose to end their lives.

nents used the slippery slope argument to claim that legalizing abortion would lead to the eugenic selection of children based on birth defects, race, or even gender. But abortion remains a practice that is used solely to alleviate unwanted pregnancies, not for the eugenic selection of who should be allowed to live. As Judge Stephen Reinhardt of the U.S. Court of Appeals for the Ninth Circuit explains, "Recognition of any right creates the possibility of abuse. [But] the slippery slope fears of [abortion] opponents have, of course, not materialized. Similarly, there is no reason to believe that legalizing assisted suicide will lead to the horrific consequences its opponents suggest."

Disbelievers in the slippery slope further argue that legalizing euthanasia and physician-assisted suicide will protect people from being abused, not put them at further risk. When people receive assistance to die in secret, there is no official safeguard or regulation to make sure they are not being abused. Conversely, Oregon's Death with Dignity Act contains more than ten safeguards to prevent abuse, which include requirements that a patient be diagnosed with a terminal illness with less than six months to live, be able to rescind their request for assistance at any time, and be certified as mentally competent. As Rob Neils, a clinical psychologist and president of the Dying Well Network, argues, "When physician aid-in-dying becomes legal and regulated, the public will be safer, not less safe!"

Whether the slippery slope exists and how far down society might fall, it will continue to be debated by opponents and supporters of euthanasia and physician-assisted suicide for a long time to come. The viewpoints presented in *Introducing Issues with Opposing Viewpoints: Euthanasia* offer insight into this and other key debates surrounding this controversial topic.

Chapter 1

Is Euthanasia Moral?

Whether it is ethical to practice euthanasia remains a matter of heated debate.

USE PLASTIC BAGS FOR SHOPPING NOT FOR KILLING

EUTHANASIA A DEAD END

Euthanasia Is Immoral

Kate Adamson

"I can assure you that my idea of what the right thing to do for an incapacitated person had drastically changed."

In the following viewpoint author Kate Adamson draws on personal experience to argue that euthanasia is immoral. In 1995 Adamson suffered a devastating stroke that for ten weeks left her with locked-in syndrome, in which a victim can think, feel, and hear but is unable to move, speak, or communicate in any way. Many of the doctors and nurses entrusted with Adamson's life did not believe she would survive, and for eight days disconnected her feeding tube in an attempt to euthanize her. Adamson argues that whatever a human being's physical or mental state, they should always be allowed access to food in order to survive. Furthermore, she points out, no one can say for sure that a patient is truly unresponsive or whether they might someday regain function, as Adamson did. She concludes that the medical industry should err on the side of life, and that brain-dead, vegetative, or other incapacitated people should be kept alive rather than being euthanized.

Kate Adamson, "Testimony of Kate Adamson for the Honorable Joseph Dunn," www.katesjourney.com, May 3, 2006. Reproduced by permission.

AS YOU READ, CONSIDER THE FOLLOWING QUESTIONS:
1. How old was Adamson when she suffered a stroke that left her with locked-in syndrome?
2. What was Adamson's reaction to having a feeding tube inserted?
3. In the author's opinion, how have euthanasia policies changed since 1995?

Most people, who will testify about this problem [of euthanasia], will be telling you about things that they have to speculate about—acting as fortune tellers. I share from my own personal experience—I have been there. I needed a feeding tube to survive and was disconnected from my feeding tube for eight days. I have suffered the pains of a supposed painless procedure. Let me assure you stopping the flow in a feeding tube is far from painless. Sadly it is a procedure practiced on the medically vulnerable, the elderly and the weak.

Every Human Deserves to Be Fed

I'd like to make two major points:

First, no one knows what they will want at the end of life—until they get there.

Second, it's very painful to starve someone and finally, feeding someone through a tube is not a heroic use of 21st century machines and science; it's a natural thing. We all need to eat or we starve and die. Starving someone is doing something that is not as many will tell you—simply not doing something. If you don't feed any living thing, you will kill it. To a person who has had a stroke the feeding tube is the equivalent of a knife and fork. If my stroke had left me unable to move my arms, would you ever have considered allowing the medical staff to forgo putting food into my mouth?

They Expected Me to Die

I learned about this issue firsthand in 1995 when I suffered a catastrophic stoke. The left side of my body is still partially paralyzed. I was once completely and totally paralyzed. I could not move at all. I could not even blink my eyes. Yet I was completely conscious, aware and able to feel pain. I had no way to communicate with anyone. I know what it is like to be hooked up to respirators, to be fed by a feeding tube—and I know what it is like to have your feeding tube turned off for eight days.

One night I was fit and healthy. A 33-year-old mother of two small toddlers with everything to live for; the next morning I was totally paralyzed. According to the doctors, I had less than one in a million chances to survive.

Ten years ago, before this happened to me, I thought I was pretty clear about what I would want if I ever suffered a catastrophic injury or illness. I was sure that I would rather die rather than be a burden to anyone. I wanted no heroic measures taken when my time came. Of course I never expected my time to come so soon. But for me it came at age 33.

As I hung on to life, for dear life, I realized how little we know about things until we have been there ourselves. We don't know what it will be like, or what we will want, until it happens to us. When I found myself in that condition, I knew that I wanted to live. As I laid there in my hospital bed listening to the doctors talk about my impending death and their plans not to treat me, I can assure you that my idea of what the right thing to do for an incapacitated person had drastically changed.

"I Felt Everything"

Let me tell you what it is like to be aware of what is going on but have to rely upon others to speak for you. When they inserted a feeding tube into my stomach, thinking I could not feel, I felt everything, but I could do nothing. I felt everything they were doing, every cut, every second. I was totally locked into my body, unable to speak, unable to move any muscle in my body. I was on life support and receiving all my food through a tube, that at one point in time was turned off for eight days and I suffered all the pains and agonies of starvation. I was in excruciating pain, in silence. I was on the inside screaming out: I DO NOT WANT TO DIE. DON'T STARVE ME. I WANT TO LIVE, FEED ME SOMETHING.

And if you asked me today if it was worth going through everything I went through to live, I would say without a doubt, and without hesitation, "Yes!"

As a disabled person my life is as important as any life. My children love me as much as any children love their parents; my husband loves me as much as when I had the full use of two good arms and two good legs. When I waged my fight to get treatment, the way life was viewed in this country was a potent weapon in my husband's fight to save me. It would not be so today.

We Must Always Err on the Side of Life

Sadly things have changed; in 1995 you just didn't do your best to speed up death. You just didn't starve people to death assuming that was a painless death. Today people do. Today courts back up selfish

Many Americans, such as these religious protesters, believe euthanasia is a form of murder.

Protesters line up outside a federal building to protest euthanasia. Opponents of euthanasia believe people should be kept alive at any cost.

disregard for human life with court orders that terminate life. The courts do not even require evidence proving the issues of life and death beyond a reasonable doubt. You can take a life if the person's life is deemed by so-called experts to be not worth living. Courts are even willing to end lives based upon pure hearsay evidence presented by people who may have good intentions or bad intentions, but nonetheless are human and fallible. This is done all the time to the disabled and the weak.

Then tell me of one case when this legislature or any courts of this land would allow you to starve to death an able-bodied male or female, yet that is just what is done in America day after day. It must stop; it is wrong. If I am wrong, then explain it to me or to the other millions of disabled people in America who, I might add, do vote.

You should never allow judges or doctors the sole and unbridled discretion to make these kinds of decisions. Give the courts clear direction forcing them to error always on the side of life, remembering that once you starve someone you can never fix the mistake. We are not asking for special rights. Disabled people don't want to be treated as special human beings. They just want to be treated as human beings.

Doctors Should Not Play God

Face the truth that starvation is cruel and painful to inflict on another human being. Face the truth that what we do for the least of our people, for the weak and infirm, for those who cannot speak for themselves marks us and defines who we are as a society.

If in your wisdom, you want to take on the role of God and you want to presume to be able to dictate death to your disabled citizens then at least have the courage to admit what you are doing. Admit that in cutting off food and water from someone, you are assisting a suicide through painful and cruel means.

EVALUATING THE AUTHORS' ARGUMENTS:

Kate Adamson draws on personal experience to argue that euthanasia is immoral. What kinds of details was she able to include because of this unique perspective? Did these details ultimately convince you to agree that euthanasia is immoral? Explain your answer.

Euthanasia Is Moral

Virginia Ironside

"It is morally reprehensible to keep alive someone who cannot see, move, speak, or hear."

In the following viewpoint Virginia Ironside argues that keeping sick people alive is immoral when they are brain-dead or suffering from a terminal illness. Ironside discusses her own mother, whose painful terminal illness was ended by euthanasia. Ironside believes that she and her doctors took mercy on her mother by allowing her torment to end. Ironside suggests that keeping seriously ill people alive is selfish and benefits families, who want to avoid losing their loved ones, at the expense of the patients, who must endure prolonged suffering. The moral thing to do, Ironside concludes, is to allow those whose quality of life has significantly deteriorated to end their pain.

Virginia Ironside is the author of newspaper columns and many books, including *Janey and Me: Growing Up with My Mother.*

AS YOU READ, CONSIDER THE FOLLOWING QUESTIONS:

1. According to the author, how did her friend react when she suggested that he end his sick wife's life?
2. After the author arranged for her mother's euthanasia, what were the last words her mother spoke?
3. According to the author, what should people fear more: death or suffering?

Virginia Ironside, "I Could Not Have Let Her Die Like This," *The Evening Standard*, April 1, 2005, p. 24. Copyright © 2005 Solo Syndication Limited. Reproduced by permission of the author.

About time too. That's what I felt when I heard that Terri Schiavo had finally died, released from years of living in a terrible half-world neither truly alive nor dead. I know it sounds callous, but it makes me furious when I hear the "keep them alive at all costs" brigade claiming the moral high ground.

"Who are we to play God?" they say. And yet they play God by interfering with a natural lifecycle and keeping some poor creature alive, with no hope of any life in the future, covered with tubes and drains, for year after painful year.

My own view is that it is morally reprehensible to keep alive someone who cannot see, move, speak or hear. The last time I was faced

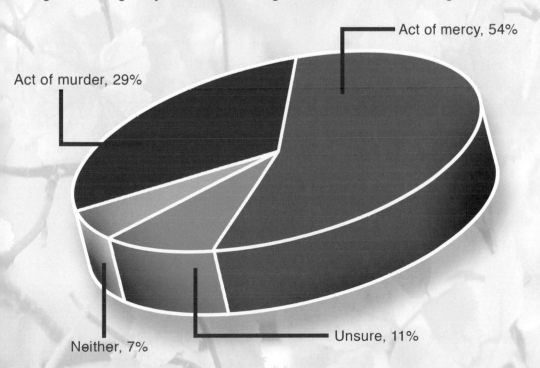

Murder or Mercy?

According to a March 2005 Fox News/Opinion Dynamics poll, 54 percent of Americans thought removing Terry Schiavo's feeding tube was the merciful thing to do.

Act of mercy, 54%

Act of murder, 29%

Neither, 7%

Unsure, 11%

Source: FOX News/Opinion Dynamics Poll, March 29–30, 2005. N = 900 registered voters nationwide. MoE ±3.

with a friend whose every organ was failing fast and who had no hope of living at all, it took moral courage to say to her husband that I thought it would be best if she were, as they say in the intensive-care units, "turned off."

Interestingly, he was grateful for my intervention, longing for someone to say what he knew was right, but what he had dared not articulate for fear of being thought beastly.

The Morality of Suffering

Terri was not on a lifesupport-system. But she was being given food and water whether she liked it or not, force-fed, not in order that she might lead a happy and fulfilled life but, rather, to draw out a state of non-being, what most of us would regard as a living hell.

I do know something about this, because my poor old mum, a woman who had tried to kill herself twice in her life. and who longed to die, found herself, at the end of her life, surrounded by doctors endlessly wanting to see if she might be suitable for bone marrow transplants, or to give her yet another blood transfusion to keep her going for another few days. She had said to me, several times (as Terri had apparently said to her husband, in her own words) that she would hate to "gutter like a candle" at the end of her life. "You will promise me you'll see to it that that won't happen?" she had asked, pitifully. I had promised.

Euthanasia Ends Suffering

But, of course, it wasn't so easy. When I first told the doctor that she wouldn't want to live in the state she was in, he gave a cheery laugh. "Oh, she may have some months yet!" he joshed, making orders for yet another transfusion. Doctors have to relieve suffering, as Terri Schiavo's did by giving her morphine until very near to her death. But what good does it do in such a miserable life?

Fifty four percent of Americans, including these protestors, believe that removing Terri Schiavo's feeding tube was an act of mercy.

Finally, a nurse came up to me one day and, with tears in her eyes, begged me to ask the doctors to do something. "I know how your mother is suffering," she said. "These doctors, they have ways (oh, I shouldn't say this, as I'm Catholic, but I beg you)." "I've already asked them!" I said. "I can't ask again. They'd think I wanted to murder her!"

But I went once again to the doctor, and this time I burst into tears and simply begged them to take some action. No one said anything, but the doctor stopped writing out the instructions he was about to give and instead pulled a prescription pad towards him. "This will help ease her pain," he said. And then he put out his hand to me. "Goodbye," he said.

When I returned to the room where my mother lay gasping, I held her hand as they gave her the injection. "Don't worry, mummy," I said. "I've organised it all. It'll just be oblivion from now on." The last words she spoke to me were: "Thank you, darling."

My mother and I were lucky. There was no government to rush through some mad bill to stop the kind of noble action that even vets carry out on animals that have no hope of reasonable life. . . .

Most Recognize the Morality of Euthanasia

In the end, I'm sure Terri's parents will acknowledge that what has been done was for the best. Most loving relatives, to be fair, do cave in after a while. Sometimes it might take days. Sometimes it might take months. Most people are generous and unselfish enough to realise that to let someone go whose future is hopeless is the kindest last act they can deliver.

I have seen doctors exercise endless patience in the ward, always being honest with the facts, guiding the relatives, ever so gently, into making the right decision themselves. Every day people are dying in hospital slightly sooner than they otherwise might, with the loving collusion of relatives and nursing staff.

And so they should be.

It was interesting that even in the States, steeped as it is in religion, the vast majority of people, according to an opinion poll, thought it was right to allow Terri to die.

Death is nothing to be frightened of. It does, after all, come to us all. It is suffering that we should be concerned about. Is there really anyone among us who would relish being kept alive in a vegetative state for years on end?

How can any loving relative imagine that our answer would ever be: "Yes"?

EVALUATING THE AUTHORS' ARGUMENTS:

In the viewpoint you just read, the author argues that forcing patients to endure a poor quality of life, rather than euthanasia, is an immoral act. Do you agree with the author that allowing patients to suffer is immoral? Are doctors morally obligated to end their patients' lives in order to end their suffering or are they obligated to preserve their patients' lives at all costs? Explain your answer.

Viewpoint 3

Euthanasia Devalues Life

Avi Shafran

"The idea of human life as sacred has become increasingly unfashionable."

In the following viewpoint Rabbi Avi Shafran argues that euthanasia is wrong because it values death over life. He worries that, by accepting euthanasia, society will embrace a culture of death in which human life is no longer considered sacred. Life will become nothing more than a commodity, he warns, which is the wrong way to view what is sacred and holy. In his view, euthanasia should be opposed because it will lead to the devaluation and disrespect of life.

Rabbi Avi Shafran is a contributor to *Jewish World Report* and the director of public affairs for Agudath Israel of America.

AS YOU READ, CONSIDER THE FOLLOWING QUESTIONS:
1. What does the word "morass" mean in the context of the viewpoint?
2. What are two examples of the way in which human life is no longer valued in America, in the author's opinion?
3. Why does the author believe that Jews in particular should be opposed to euthanasia?

Avi Shafran, "Suicide Watch," *Jewish World Review,* www.jewishworldreview.com, January 24, 2006. Reproduced by permission.

I n *The New England Journal of Medicine* [in 2005], two Dutch physicians published a set of guidelines for infant euthanasia; one of the doctors has admitted to presiding over the killing of at least four babies, by means of a lethal intravenous drip of morphine and midazolam (a sleeping agent). Although 12-year-olds in Holland already can, with their parents' approval, legally enlist doctors to kill them, the dispatching of sick babies remains illegal under Dutch law; the doctors hope that their proposed guidelines will provide a legal basis for such endeavors.

In the meanwhile, Belgium has enacted a euthanasia law similar to that of the Netherlands.

Life Is Sacred

To some, this all is just the march of progress. In the eyes of Judaism, though, it is a descent into a deep moral morass.

Suicide is regarded by Jewish law as a sin, and helping a patient— even one who two doctors agree is likely to die within six months, whom

Many find euthanasia hard to reconcile with religious beliefs that teach every life is sacred.

"He won the right to die without dignity."

Oregon's law permits abetting—to kill himself is acting as an accessory to the taking of a life. All the Torah's laws, in fact, with the exception only of three cardinal ones (idolatry, sexual immorality and murder), are put aside when life—even for a limited period—is in the balance.

Contemporary society, unfortunately, has a very different take.

A Culture that Devalues Life

From the nearly non-stop portrayals of death and violence in what passes for contemporary "entertainment" to the all-too-real carnage on our cities' streets, the idea of human life as sacred has become increasingly unfashionable. In a world where youngsters regularly murder for a car, a pair of shoes or even just "for fun," or where women routinely decide to stop an unborn baby's heart to accommodate their own personal or professional goals, an elderly or infirm person's life just doesn't command the *consequence* it once did.

Nor have elements of the "intelligentsia" been hesitant to assist in human life's devaluation.

Peter Singer, for example, the famed Professor of Bioethics at Princeton University's Center for Human Values, has proposed the termination (even without niceties like consent) of what he calls "miserable beings"—people whose lives he deems devoid of pleasure.

Asked by *The New York Times* recently what idea, value or institution

FAST FACT

A series of National Opinion Research Center General Social Surveys that span three decades show that those who approve of euthanasia are also more likely to approve of suicide and abortion.

the world takes for granted today he thinks may disappear in the next 35 years, Professor Singer responded: "the traditional view of the sanctity of human life," which, he maintained, "will collapse under pressure from scientific, technological and demographic developments."

On another occasion, he went further still, predicting that once society jettisons "doctrines about the sanctity of human life," it will be "the *refusal,* to accept killing that, in some cases, [will be seen as] horrific."

We're not there, yet. But even in the United States, where there remains considerable public aversion for assisted suicide and euthanasia, doctors report that both occur in hospitals much more frequently than most of us realize.

The elderly and diseased are rapidly increasing in number. Modern medicine has increased longevity and provided cures for many once-fatal illnesses. Add skyrocketing insurance costs and the resultant fiscal crisis in health care, and life runs the risk of becoming less a holy, divine gift than. . . a commodity.

And every businessman knows how important it is to turn over one's stock, to clear out the old and make way for the new. . . .

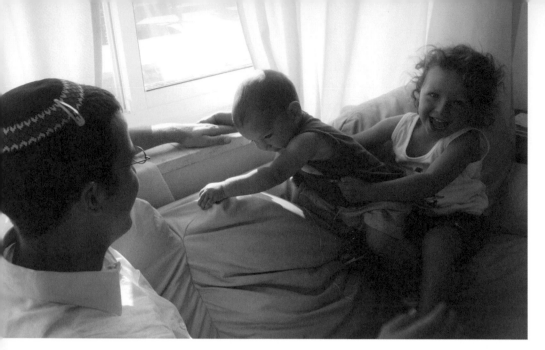

Some believe that American Jews should eschew euthanasia in favor of choosing a philosophy of life.

Life Must Be Defended

American Jews, in consonance with their religious heritage, should be at the forefront of "choosing life."

In ancient cultures that celebrated paganism and immorality, our ancestors stood up and apart.

In the midst of a culture that devalues human life, we should be doing no less.

EVALUATING THE AUTHORS' ARGUMENTS:

In this viewpoint Shafran argues that euthanasia is just one example of how American culture does not value life. Do you agree with this charge? In what ways do you think American culture values or does not value life? Explain your answer.

Viewpoint

4

Euthanasia Does Not Devalue Life

"To insist on artificially maintaining existence without regard for its condition is a degradation of the meaning of life, not a promotion of it."

Jay Werbinox Taylor

In the following viewpoint Jay Werbinox Taylor explains why he believes that euthanasia does not devalue life. Taylor makes a distinction between life and merely being alive, which is the state some coma or PVS [persistent vegetative state] patients are kept in by machines. In Taylor's view, being kept physically alive when one's quality of life has disintegrated to the point of being unable to function independently is not right. He concludes that death is a natural part of life, and allowing a person to slip away naturally is respectful of the life he or she lived.

Jay Werbinox Taylor once ran for the House of Representatives in Georgia. He is a regular guest writer for various journals and magazines, including *American Atheist*, from which this viewpoint was taken.

AS YOU READ, CONSIDER THE FOLLOWING QUESTIONS:

1. What is the author's opinion of labels such as "culture of life" or "culture of death"?
2. According to the author, what constitutes sadism in regard to euthanasia?
3. What does the author say that people must do out of respect for life?

To those who thought the whole Terri Schiavo drama was over, think again. The whole issue is being cast into so many molds that soon it will be about—everything! It contains God, religion, state's rights, the role of the federal government, as well as definitions of life, and the right to die. Many of those who openly opposed the removal of her feeding tube claim to represent a "culture of life," and some have branded those who supported her husband's right to allow her to die as members of a "culture of death.". . .

Prolonging Life Can Sometimes Be Degrading

What about Terri's wishes? This is the real issue. Whether she made her thoughts clear to her husband or not will never be known by us, but if it indeed was her wish to be allowed to die rather than linger in a vegetative state, who would deny her this right, and why? Would

Americans rally in front of a federal building to demonstrate about euthanasia, one of America's most contentious political issues.

the so called "proponents of life," who overlook the difference between mere existence and actual living, have continued to force Terri
to linger even if they had known it was her desire to be set free? If so,
where is their much vaunted concern for her?

To invent religiously and politically charged labels such as "a

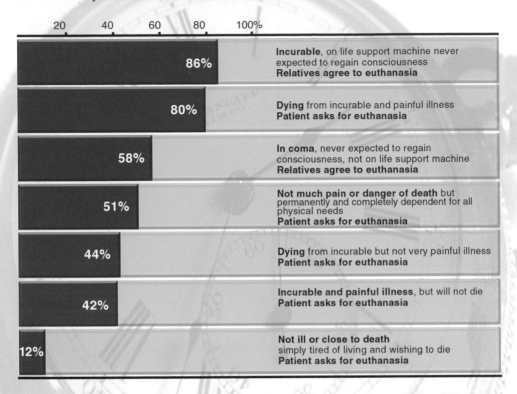

Varying Degrees of Euthanasia

Percentage of British citizens who think euthanasia should definitely or probably be allowed by law for those who are:

Percentage	Description
86%	**Incurable**, on life support machine never expected to regain consciousness **Relatives agree to euthanasia**
80%	**Dying** from incurable and painful illness **Patient asks for euthanasia**
58%	**In coma**, never expected to regain consciousness, not on life support machine **Relatives agree to euthanasia**
51%	**Not much pain or danger of death** but permanently and completely dependent for all physical needs **Patient asks for euthanasia**
44%	**Dying** from incurable but not very painful illness **Patient asks for euthanasia**
42%	**Incurable and painful illness**, but will not die **Patient asks for euthanasia**
12%	**Not ill or close to death** simply tired of living and wishing to die **Patient asks for euthanasia**

Source: David Donnison, "Not Just an Issue of Life and Death—the British Social Attitudes Survey," www.euthanasia.cc/97-1dvd.html.

culture of life" accomplishes nothing without distinguishing the difference between life and mere survival. To insist on artificially maintaining existence without regard for its condition is a degradation of the meaning of life, not a promotion of it. To do so against the wishes of the individual involved is sadism, not compassion.

Respecting Life Requires Honoring Death

Life and death are inseparable. One will never exist without the other. Out of respect for life itself we must honor death for those who are no longer able to live it with any hope of recovery or joy. Those who love life understand this, and those who do not fear death understand it as well. Why is it that those who most demonstrably claim to support "life," yet who equally praise death as going to a "better place," are the ones who are having the hardest time with it?

It is instructive that those who praise death as a reunion with God were among those who were willing to do anything to prevent it for Terri Schiavo. They preach that the glories of the Spirit are above this world, yet strive with all their power to prevent death for someone who lingers in a hopeless vegetative state, and betray their actual fear of death in the process. It is this fear of death that fuels their obsession with it. It is not a mystery that those who most fear death require the most faith, and those who make the greatest displays of their faith have little to no faith at all.

EVALUATING THE AUTHORS' ARGUMENTS:

The author of this viewpoint published his article in *American Atheist*, a magazine that considers issues from an atheistic perspective. The author of the previous viewpoint is a rabbi, a religious leader in the Jewish faith. How does knowing the authors' different backgrounds help you interpret their opposing views on euthanasia?

Chapter 2

Who Should Receive Euthanasia?

Whether euthanasia endangers the disabled, the elderly and other groups is a matter of ongoing debate.

Euthanasia Should Sometimes Be Applied to Children

Jim Holt

"To keep alive an infant whose short life expectancy will be dominated by pain [is] to do that infant a continuous injury."

In the following viewpoint Jim Holt argues that society has a moral obligation to euthanize babies born with very severe birth defects. He considers the dilemma of badly deformed children who are born with missing body parts or even without pieces of their brains. He argues that while it is technically possible to keep them alive artificially, they will never enjoy normal human lives. In other cases, babies suffering from extreme illness, disease, or birth defects will have very short life expectancies that will only be filled with pain and suffering. For these reasons, Holt concludes that society has a moral obligation to relieve the suffering of such babies by euthanizing them.

Jim Holt is the author of the "Egghead" column for Slate.com, and frequently contributes to publications such as the *New Yorker* and the *New York Times Magazine*, from which this viewpoint was taken.

AS YOU READ, CONSIDER THE FOLLOWING QUESTIONS:

1. Explain the condition of anencephaly, as described by the author.
2. What is the main idea behind the Groningen protocol, according to the author?
3. Instead of the duty to treat all life as sacred, what new moral duty does the author say should be upheld?

I nfanticide—the deliberate killing of newborns with the consent of the parents and the community—has been common throughout most of human history. In some societies, like the Eskimos, the Kung in Africa and 18th-century Japan, it served as a form of birth control when food supplies were limited. In others, like the Greek city-states and ancient Rome, it was a way of getting rid of deformed babies. (Plato was an ardent advocate of infanticide for eugenic purposes.) But the three great monotheistic religions, Judaism, Christianity and Islam, all condemned infanticide as murder, holding that only God has the right to take innocent human life. Consequently, the practice has long been outlawed in every Western nation.

FAST FACT

Approximately one to two thousand babies in the United States are born each year with anencephaly, a serious birth defect in which part of the brain fails to develop. About 95 percent of women who learn that they will have an anencephalic baby choose to abort the fetus.

Examining Infant Euthanasia

This year, however, a new chapter may have begun in the history of infanticide. Two physicians practicing in the Netherlands, the very heart of civilized Europe, this spring published in *The New England Journal of Medicine* a set of guidelines for what they called infant "euthanasia." The authors named their guidelines the Groningen protocol, after the city where they work. One of the physicians, Dr. Eduard Verhagen, has admitted to presiding over the killing of four babies in the last three years, by means of a lethal intravenous drip of morphine and midazolam (a sleeping agent). While Verhagen's ac-

Plato, depicted here surrounded by students, was an advocate of infanticide. He believed it could help weed out genetically undesirable people.

tions were illegal under Dutch law, he hasn't been prosecuted for them; and if his guidelines were to be accepted, they could establish a legal basis for his death-administering work.

At first blush, a call for open infanticide would seem to be the opposite of moral progress. It offends against the "sanctity of life," a doctrine that has come to suffuse moral consciousness, especially in the United States. All human life is held to be of equal and inestimable value. A newborn baby, no matter how deformed or retarded, has a right to life—a right that trumps all other moral considerations. Violating that right is always and everywhere murder.

Is Life Always Worth Living?

The sanctity-of-life doctrine has an impressively absolute ring to it. In practice, however, it has proved quite flexible. Take the case of a baby who is born missing most or all of its brain. This condition, known as anencephaly, occurs in about 1 in every 2,000 births. An anencephalic baby, while biologically human, will never develop a rudimentary consciousness, let alone an ability to relate to others or a sense of the future. Yet according to the sanctity-of-life doctrine,

This severely handicapped boy can barely function by himself. Supporters of infanticide believe it is merciful to euthanize severely handicapped children.

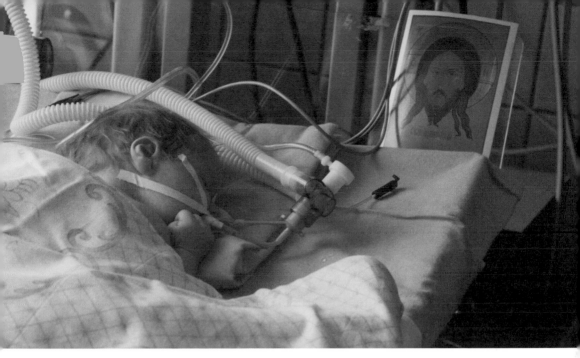

In the Netherlands, euthanasia is legal for infants with severe disabilities, such as children who are born missing pieces of their brain.

those deficiencies do not affect its moral status and hence its right to life. Anencephalic babies could be kept alive for years, given the necessary life support. Yet treatment is typically withheld from them on the grounds that it amounts to "extraordinary means"—even though a baby with a normal brain in need of similar treatment would not be so deprived. Thus they are allowed to die. . . .

It is interesting to contrast the sort of passive euthanasia of infants that is deemed acceptable in our sanctity-of-life culture with the active form that has been advocated in the Netherlands. The Groningen protocol is concerned with an element not present in the above cases: unbearable and unrelievable suffering. Consider the case of Sanne, a Dutch baby girl who was born with a severe form of Hallopeau-Siemens syndrome, a rare skin disease. As reported earlier this year by Gregory Crouch in the *Times*, the baby Sanne's "skin would literally come off if anyone touched her, leaving painful scar tissue in its place." With this condition, she was expected to live at most 9 or 10 years before dying of skin cancer. Her parents asked that an end be put to her ordeal, but hospital officials, fearing criminal prosecution, refused. After six months of agony, Sanne finally died of pneumonia.

In a case like Sanne's, a new moral duty would seem to be germane: the duty to prevent suffering, especially futile suffering. That is what the Groningen protocol seeks to recognize. If the newborn's prognosis is hopeless and the pain both severe and unrelievable, it observes, the parents and physicians "may concur that death would be more humane than continued life." The protocol aims to safeguard against "unjustified" euthanasia by offering a checklist of requirements, including informed consent of both parents, certain diagnosis, confirmation by at least one independent doctor and so on.

The debate over infant euthanasia is usually framed as a collision between two values: sanctity of life and quality of life. Judgments about the latter, of course, are notoriously subjective and can lead you down a slippery slope. But shifting the emphasis to suffering changes the terms of the debate. To keep alive an infant whose short life expectancy will be dominated by pain—pain that it can neither bear nor comprehend—is, it might be argued, to do that infant a continuous injury.

Our sense of what constitutes moral progress is a matter partly of reason and partly of sentiment. On the reason side, the Groningen protocol may seem progressive because it refuses to countenance the prolonging of an infant's suffering merely to satisfy a dubious distinction between "killing" and "letting nature take its course." It insists on unflinching honesty about a practice that is often shrouded in casuistry in the United States.

EVALUATING THE AUTHORS' ARGUMENTS:

Jim Holt began his essay by explaining how Judaism, Christianity, and Islam have long outlawed the killing of infants. Yet Holt goes on to argue that it should be permissible to euthanize some infants. With this in mind, explain why you think Holt chose to begin his essay the way he did. What point was he attempting to make with such an introduction? Do you think he was successful? Explain your answer.

Euthanasia Must Never Be Applied to Children

George Neumayr

"What is the difference between aborting a baby and euthanizing it? Nothing except the timing of the killing."

In the following viewpoint George Neumayr argues that euthanasia should never be performed on people who cannot consent to the procedure, such as newborn children. He discusses the Groningen protocol, a controversial law permitting doctors in the Netherlands to euthanize patients, including babies, who are born with defects. He views the doctors who perform such procedures as inhumane and barbaric because they rob a child of life without that child's permission, and put themselves in the position of deciding whose life is worth living. Neumayr concludes that even if parents and doctors think that relieving the child's suffering would be preferable to life, children must never be euthanized because it violates their rights.

George Neumayr is executive editor of the *American Spectator*, from which this viewpoint was taken.

AS YOU READ, CONSIDER THE FOLLOWING QUESTIONS:

1. When did Holland legalize euthanasia for adults, as reported by the author?
2. Who is Eduard Verhagen?
3. What does the author mean when he describes euthanasia as "an act of annoyance"?

What is the difference between aborting a baby and euthanizing it? Nothing except the timing of the killing. In the Netherlands, a country that never hesitates to unfold the logic of liberalism to its farthest points, doctors have devised a program to euthanize babies deemed defective. They euthanized four babies [in 2004], according to press reports. Now they are calling upon the Dutch government to pursue a more ambitious program that

A Dutch citizen protests her country's acceptance of infant euthanasia on the grounds it is immoral and unfair.

would let doctors euthanize undesirables with "no free will," meaning minors.

Children Can't Speak for Themselves

C.S. Lewis wrote that evil is done "in clean, carpeted, warmed and well-lighted offices, by quiet men with white collars and cut fingernails and smooth-shaven cheeks who do not need to raise their voices." Lewis could have added that they don't even need to raise their voices when they go on public radio to explain their evil. [In December 2004] National Public Radio politely interviewed one of the Dutch doctors overseeing the euthanasia-for-children program, Eduard Verhagen, clinical director of the Pediatric Clinic of the University Hospital at Groningen. This white-coated doctor with neatly trimmed fingernails didn't need to raise his voice when asked by NPR quite casually, "How was it decided that they should die?" The children had medical conditions like "spina bifida," responded Verhagen. The babies were born "with incurable conditions," so "we felt that in these children the most humane course of action would be to allow the child to die, and even actively assist them in their death."

FAST FACT

According to an article in the *New England Journal of Medicine*, approximately six hundred of the two hundred thousand infants born in the Netherlands each year die as a result of euthanasia.

Assist them in their death. Had the toddlers scrawled out a consent form? No, they lack "free will," so pediatricians made the decision for them. Asked if what his hospital had done was legal, Verhagen blithely said, "No, it's not legal," but implied the Dutch government would tidy up that decision later. "It's a very delicate and very important decision that one needs to make," he said. "And if such a decision is made, we prefer to have it tested or assessed by a committee of experts, just to make sure that we have taken into account all the requirements and that we are really doing something that is correct."

Would parents be able to veto the decision on which children get to live or die according to the committee? Apparently not. When

Opponents of infanticide, such as these religious protestors, believe that infants should not be euthanized because they are unable to make the decision themselves.

Verhagen was asked, "Is it just up to the parents?" he said, "No." But he quickly caught himself and magnanimously allowed that parents are "always very much involved." Ultimately, however, who lives or dies is the culture's decision, he said. "Let's see how society thinks of it," he offered. "What we would like to happen here in Holland is that we put the spotlight on such decisions because they need to be extremely secure. And instead of taking these decisions in a kind of gray area, we want them to be in the spotlight. . . . The culture in Holland is a culture where euthanasia for adults has been legalized in 2002 by the Parliament."

Verhagen concluded on the thought that "the best way to protect life is to sometimes assist a little bit in death." This contradicted what he had said earlier when he stressed that "we are actually talking about children that are already in a dying process." No, they were not dying. If they were dying, they would have died without euthanasia. It is precisely because they were not dying that the Dutch doctors euthanized them.

We Must Stop These Barbaric Acts

Euthanasia isn't letting a patient die but killing a patient who isn't dying. It is an act of annoyance at a patient who isn't dying on the

A crowd gathers at the Dutch Senate to protest the Groningen protocol, the Dutch law that allows the euthanasia of children.

timetable those who want the patient to die would prefer. In the Terri Schiavo case, for example, her impatient husband demanded that she be deprived of food and water because she wasn't dying with sufficient speed. "Has she died yet?" a nurse heard him say. "When is that bitch going to die?" Euthanasia, it was said, would allow Schiavo to "die in peace." Die in peace? No, it would guarantee that she die violently. Starvation is not a peaceful act.

In clean, well-lighted hospitals, Verhagen and doctors like him are committing barbaric acts no different from pagans of old leaving inconvenient children on hilltops. Whenever a doctor uses the word "humane," it is clear that he has already performed the inhuman.

EVALUATING THE AUTHORS' ARGUMENTS:

In this viewpoint George Neumayr argues that euthanizing children is barbaric and inhumane. In the previous viewpoint Jim Holt argues that euthanizing children is merciful and humane. Which argument did you find more convincing? Why? Support your answer using evidence from the text.

Viewpoint
3

People in a Persistent Vegetative State Should Be Allowed to Die

Robert D. Orr

"There are clearly situations where a feeding tube must be used. There are other situations where a feeding tube would be morally wrong."

In the following viewpoint Robert Orr argues that feeding tubes should be removed from patients who are in a permanent vegetative state (PVS), even if the patient has not made it known whether he or she wishes to be kept alive by a feeding tube. Orr reasons that even though PVS patients are technically alive and can be kept alive for a long time, life is finite and must not always be preserved beyond a certain point. Because there is usually little hope that a PVS patient will recover, and his or her remaining life will be a continuous struggle, Orr believes that doctors may discontinue what he calls "death-postponing treatment," such as a feeding tube, in order to allow the patient to die. While religious principles might lead people to declare that all life is sacred, Orr concludes that technology requires that human beings must make choices about death.

Orr is the director of ethics for Fletcher Allen Health Care and professor of family medicine at the University of Vermont College of Medicine.

AS YOU READ, CONSIDER THE FOLLOWING QUESTIONS:
1. What does the author mean when he says that a PVS patient is "awake but unaware"?
2. In Orr's opinion, why should PVS patients be compared to a patient with liver failure rather than a newborn infant?
3. According to Orr, what types of cases are usually not treated because the burden is disproportionate to the benefit?

T he cases we read about in the newspaper—in which families are divided and court battles fought—most often involve patients in a permanent vegetative state (PVS). This is a condition of permanent unawareness most often caused by severe head injury or by the brain being deprived of oxygen for several minutes. . . . In a PVS patient, the heart, lungs, kidneys, and other organs continue to function; given good nursing care and artificially administered fluids and nutrition, a person can live in this permanent vegetative state for many years.

Conscious or Unconscious?

A person in a PVS may still have reflexes from the spinal cord (grasping, withdrawal from pain) or the brain stem (breathing, regulation of blood pressure), including the demonstration of sleep-wake cycles. He may "sleep" for several hours, then "awaken" for a while; the eyes are open and wander about, but do not fix on or follow objects. The person in a PVS is "awake, but unaware" because the areas of the upper brain that allow a person to perceive his or her environment and to act voluntarily are no longer functioning.

Some of the clinical controversy about nutritional support for persons in a PVS is due to uncertainty. After a head injury or resuscitation from a cardiac arrest, it may be several weeks or months before a patient can rightly be declared to be in a PVS—months during which

Most Americans Would Want to Be Allowed to Die

The majority of Americans would not want to be kept alive if they were in a coma or a persistent vegetative state, according to an April 2005 Harris Poll.

The poll asked the respondents the following question:

If you were filling out a living will, what directions would you give your doctor in the event you became unconscious, and, to a reasonable degree of medical certainty, you would never regain consciousness?

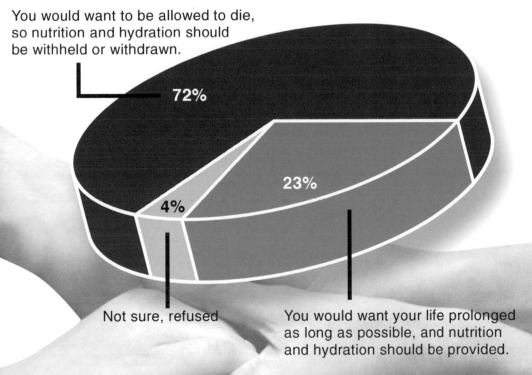

You would want to be allowed to die, so nutrition and hydration should be withheld or withdrawn.

72%

4%

23%

Not sure, refused

You would want your life prolonged as long as possible, and nutrition and hydration should be provided.

Note: Percentages may not add up to 100 percent due to rounding

Source: Majorities of U.S. Adults Favor Euthanasia and Physician-Assisted Suicide by More than Two-to-One, www.harrisinteractive.com, April 27, 2005.

the provision of nutritional support via feeding tubes is often very appropriate. Loved ones usually remain optimistic, hoping for improvement, praying for full recovery. The length of time from brain damage to declaration of a PVS can extend, depending on the cause of the brain injury, from one month to twelve months. And just to muddy the waters even further, there are rare instances of delayed improvement after many months or even a few years, so that the previously unaware patient regains some ability to perceive his or her environment, and may even be able to say a few words. These individuals are now in a "minimally conscious state." More than minimal delayed improvement is exceedingly rare. . . .

The greatest ethical dilemma surrounding the use or non-use of nutritional support for persons in a PVS arises from the fact that they are not clearly dying. With good nursing care and nutrition, individuals in this condition have survived for up to thirty-five years. Those who advocate continued nutritional support argue thus: this person is alive and not actively or imminently dying; it is possible to keep him alive with minimal effort; this human life is sacred; therefore we are obligated to continue to give artificially administered fluids and nutrition.

No Potential for Recovery

It is hard to disagree with the various steps in this line of reasoning. . . . Let us stipulate the following: the person in a PVS is alive; he can be kept alive for a long time; his life is sacred. But does the obligation to maintain that severely compromised human life necessarily follow from these premises?

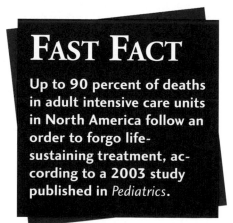

Let's first address the issue of whether he is dying. One could maintain that his physical condition is such that he will die soon but for the artificial provision of fluids and nutrition. Thus the permanent vegetative state could be construed to be lethal in and of itself. However, that fatal outcome is not inevitable since the saving treatment is simple. How does this differ from the imperative to provide nourishment for a newborn who would die without the provision of fluids and nutrition? There are two differences. Most new-

FAST FACT

Up to 90 percent of deaths in adult intensive care units in North America follow an order to forgo life-sustaining treatment, according to a 2003 study published in *Pediatrics*.

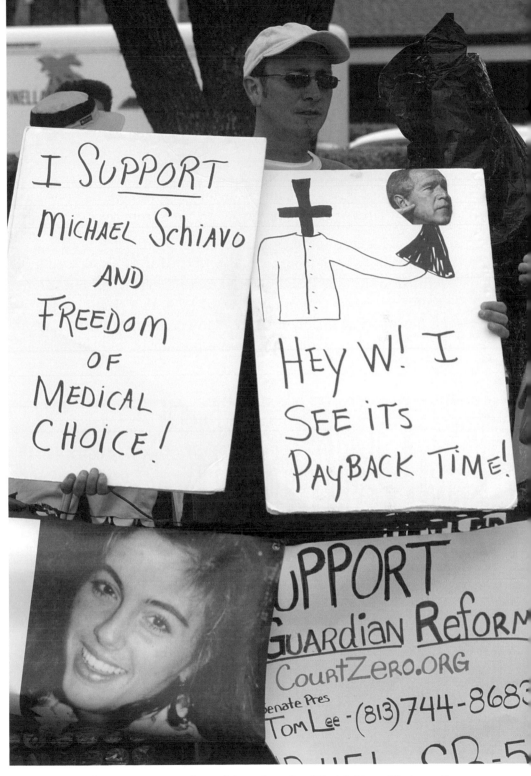

Tensions run high at one protest in favor of the euthanasia of Terri Schiavo. The issue of whether Schiavo should be kept alive polarized the nation in 2005.

borns are able to take in nutrition if it is placed in or near their mouths. PVS patients can't swallow, so the nutrition must be delivered further down the gastrointestinal tract. As for sick or premature infants, they have a great potential for improvement, growth, and development. The PVS patient has no such potential.

Rather than a newborn, a better analogy for this aspect of the discussion would be a person with kidney failure. The kidney failure itself is life-threatening, but it is fairly easily corrected by dialysis three times a week. If the person has another condition that renders him unaware of his surroundings, or a condition that makes life a continuous difficult struggle, most would agree that the person is ethically permitted to stop the dialysis even if that means he will not survive. The ultimate cause of death was treatable, so that death could have been postponed, possibly for years. However, other mitigating circumstances may make the dialysis disproportionate, and so one should

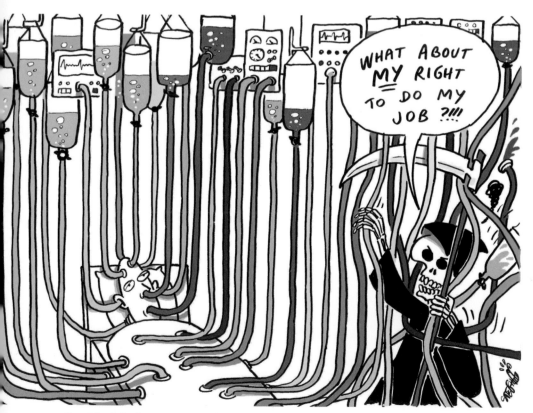

Copyright © Stephane Peray. Reproduced by permission of Cagle Cartoons, Inc.

be allowed to discontinue this death-postponing treatment in a person who is not imminently dying.

Life Must Not Always Be Preserved

Does the sanctity of life, a basic tenet of Christianity, Judaism, and Islam, dictate that life must always be preserved if it is humanly possible to do so? Our moral intuitions tell us the answer is no.

It might be possible to postpone the death of a patient from end-stage heart failure by doing one more resuscitation. It might be possible to postpone the death of someone with end-stage liver disease by doing a liver transplant. It might be possible to postpone the death of someone with painful cancer with a few more blood transfusions or another round of chemotherapy. But these therapies are often not used—because the burden is disproportionate to the benefit. Thus the timing of death is often a matter of choice. In fact, it is commonly accepted that the timing of 80 percent of deaths that occur in a hospital is chosen.

Believers do not like to use the words "choice" and "death" in the same sentence. Doing so recalls acrimonious contests about the "right to life" versus the "right to choose" that are the pivotal point in debates about abortion, assisted suicide, and euthanasia. And certainly belief in the sanctity of human life obligates believers to forgo some choices. But does this belief preclude all choices? No: life is full of difficult choices. This is true for believers and nonbelievers alike. Believers may have more guidance about what choices to make and perhaps some limits on options, but we still are faced with many choices—such as choices about the use or non-use of feeding tubes. . . .

Life Is Finite

If belief in the sanctity of human life translated automatically into an obligation to preserve each human life at all costs, we would not have to debate proportionate and disproportionate treatments. We would simply be obligated to use all treatments available until they failed to work. However, . . . human life is finite. All of us will die. Since that is inevitable, God expects us to care wisely for our own bodies and for those of our loved ones, and also for our resources. Healthcare professionals similarly must be wise stewards of their skills and services.

Taking into consideration the scriptural principle of stewardship and the tradition of proportionate treatment, I conclude that there must be some degree of discretion in the use or non-use of feeding tubes. There are clearly situations where a feeding tube must be used. There are other situations where a feeding tube would be morally wrong.

EVALUATING THE AUTHORS' ARGUMENTS:

In this viewpoint Robert D. Orr argues that no matter how sacred life is considered to be, medical technology often creates situations in which people must make a choice about death. Explain what he means by this point. In your opinion, is it possible to make a choice about death and still consider life to be sacred? Why or why not?

People in a Persistent Vegetative State Should Not Be Allowed to Die

Fred Rosner

"Feeding tubes and hydration are part and parcel of supportive care . . . [and] should not be abandoned if doing so would hasten the patient's death."

In the following viewpoint Fred Rosner argues that it is morally wrong to allow patients in a persistent vegetative state (PVS) to die, even if the courts and the American Medical Association have approved such a practice. He laments that nutrition and hydration, which used to be standard care for PVS patients, are now considered life-prolonging treatment. Rosner believes that all human life is always valuable and should never be taken. In his view, all life belongs to God, so people do not have the right to take one another's lives, or even to take their own life.

Rosner is a teaching attending physician for Mount Sinai Services at Elmhurst Hospital Center and a professor of medicine at Mount Sinai School of Medicine.

Fred Rosner, "Death by Withdrawal of Nutrition and Hydration," *The Einstein Journal of Biology and Medicine*, vol. 20, 2004, pp. 81–84. Copyright © 2004. Reproduced by permission of the author.

AS YOU READ, CONSIDER THE FOLLOWING QUESTIONS:
1. When did the AMA begin to endorse limited use of euthanasia?
2. What does the author mean when he writes that a life with suffering is preferable to death?
3. What constitutes supportive care, as described by the author?

I n a landmark statement in March 1986, the American Medical Association's (AMA) Council on Ethical and Judicial affairs announced that, in certain limited circumstances life prolonging medical treatment, including "medication and artificially or technologically applied respiration, nutrition or hydration" may be stopped or withheld. There is today nearly universal support in the medical, legal, ethical, and lay

Sodium pentothal, a drug that is part of these euthanasia kits, paralyzes a person's nervous system and brings on death.

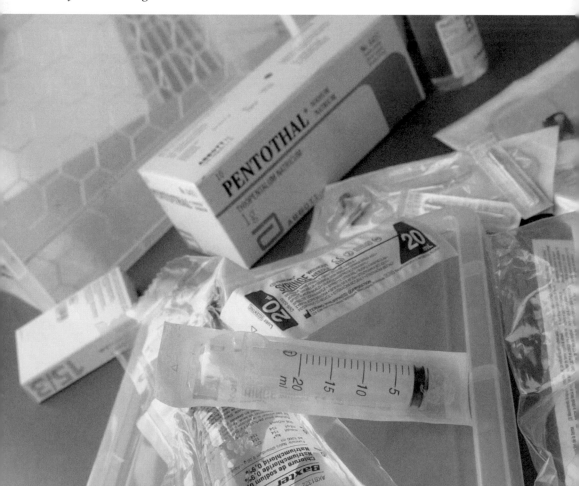

professions for this AMA position. A small minority at the AMA objected, saying, "This is a grievous error because death by starvation, dehydration, volume depletion, or a combination of these is not death from the underlying disease processes and could be considered euthanasia." Others in the minority argued that this development bears the seeds of a great potential abuse since pulling the tube or pulling the plug are the equivalent of euthanasia which is illegal in the United States. I thus interpret the differences of opinion to hinge on whether feeding tubes and hydration are medical treatments and when appropriate may be ethically and legally withheld or withdrawn. Alternately, feeding tubes and hydration are part and parcel of supportive care, such as turning the patient, singing, reading, talking or just listening to the patient who is dying. These general supportive measures should not be abandoned if doing so would hasten the patient's death.

Every Moment Is Worth Something

In the Judas-Christian [sic] system of ethics and values, human life is considered to be of infinite and inestimable value. Therefore, one could argue philosophically that every moment of a person's life is also

A group of disabled Americans protests euthanasia. Some disabled Americans worry their lives could be viewed as not worth living by those who are in favor of the practice.

of supreme value. Furthermore, a person's life and body are not his own property to do with as he wishes. The proprietor of all life including human life is none other than God Himself.

My colleague, friend, mentor, and consultant, Rabbi J. David Bleich, visiting Professor of Law at Yeshiva University's Cardozo Law School, told me personal privilege as well as personal responsibility with regard to the human body and human life are similar to the privilege and responsibility of a bailee with regard to a bailment with which he has been entrusted. It is the duty of a bailee who has accepted an object of value for safekeeping to safeguard the bailment and to return it to its rightful owner upon demand. Man is but a steward over his human body and is charged with its preservation. He must abide by the limitations placed upon his rights of use and enjoyment.

Moral Obligations to Life

Life with suffering is regarded as being, in many cases, preferable to termination of life and with it elimination of suffering. Life accompanied by pain may be preferable to death. It may serve as atonement for the dying person. It may serve to stimulate feelings of compassion and altruism among the family members and caregivers or even the recognition of their own mortality. These feelings may facilitate their own fulfillment of the divine plan of creation. Even when the life of a person on his deathbed seems to be devoid of benefit, meaning or purpose, the patient retains unique human value by virtue of the role he plays in providing an opportunity of love and compassion. Human life represents a purpose in and of itself (i.e., sheer human existence is endowed with moral value).

Many people may disagree with Rabbi Bleich's view, which is based on theological ethics and teachings, which may at times appear to be rigorous, and fail to achieve acceptance in a secular society. Nevertheless, concludes Rabbi Bleich, an understanding and appreciation of these traditions may result in the tempering of some of the rather extreme views about end-of-life issues such as active euthanasia and physician assisted suicide that are currently in vogue. If some doubt is engendered in the minds of physicians and other caregivers tending to the needs of the terminally ill, they may take to heart the fact that if they are to err, better to err on the side of life.

My own view is that even if the courts and secular ethicists sanction the withholding or withdrawal of fluids and nutrition from the terminally ill and from chronic vegetative state patients, what is legal and socially acceptable is not always moral and merciful. The patient's or family's right of starving or dehydrating the patient to death does not mean that starvation and/or dehydration are right. The medical literature is divided about whether or not death by starvation and/or dehydration is more painful and induces more suffering than death with full nutrition and hydration. Finally, legal permissibility by court order to induce death by removing or withholding food and hydration is not necessarily synonymous with moral license to do so.

EVALUATING THE AUTHORS' ARGUMENTS:

In this viewpoint Fred Rosner argues that a life with suffering is preferable to no life at all, and that PVS patients have a lot to offer the people around them. Do you agree with Rosner's point that suffering can be valuable? Why or why not?

Chapter 3

Should Physician-Assisted Suicide Be Legal?

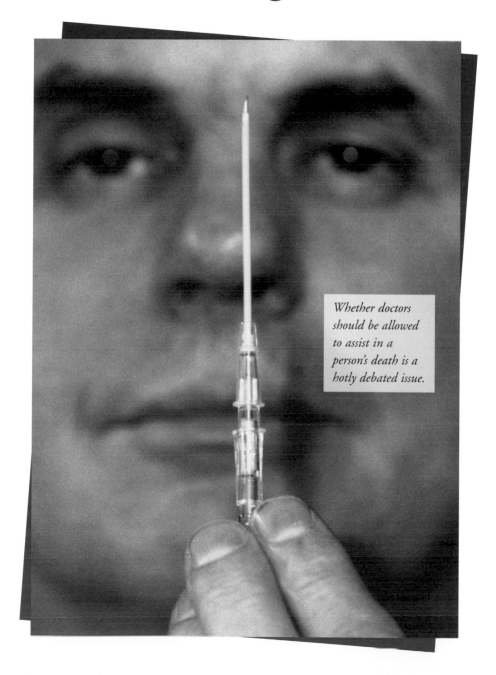

Whether doctors should be allowed to assist in a person's death is a hotly debated issue.

Physician-Assisted Suicide Should Be Legal

"Those who happen to live in Oregon . . . have a kind of insurance the rest of us don't: They know they can get out of life when they are desperate to do so."

Betty Rollin

In the following viewpoint Betty Rollin argues that physician-assisted suicide (PAS) should be legal. She claims that PAS allows terminally ill patients to end their lives with dignity and a sense of well-being. Rollin describes three patients, including her own mother, whose final days, weeks, or years were greatly improved by having the option to end their own lives. As long as PAS remains illegal, she argues, terminally ill patients are forced to break the law, to have their loved ones break the law, and to die without control.

Rollin serves on the board of directors of the Death with Dignity National Center, and she is the author of *Last Wish*.

AS YOU READ, CONSIDER THE FOLLOWING QUESTIONS:
1. According to the author, why do many terminally ill people not attempt to take their own lives?

Betty Rollin, "Path to a Peaceful Death," *The Washington Post*, May 30, 2004, p. B7. © 2004 The Washington Post Company. Reproduced by permission of the author.

2. How many people does the author say use Oregon's assisted suicide law each year?
3. What made the author's mother change her behavior toward the end of her life?

When I helped my mother die in 1983, there was no Oregon. That is, there was no state where physician-assisted suicide was legal. Not that it would have mattered because the law applies only to residents of Oregon and my mother lived in New York. So we were on our own, the three of us: my mother, who was dying of ovarian cancer but in her view not fast enough; my

Under Oregon's physician-assisted suicide law, terminally ill patients are prescribed a lethal medication that they take in the comfort of their home.

husband, and I, my mother's only child. Amateur criminals all. But we muddled through. She got the pills down. She slipped away gratefully, gracefully, peacefully.

Many Obstacles

So it worked for us, but it might not have. Many terminally ill people who want to die try and fail and wind up suffering more than they did before. But in most cases, they don't even try. They're too weak or don't have the means to end their lives themselves, and their loved ones are too frightened to help. Not unreasonable since assisted suicide is illegal. If you're a physician and help a patient die, you lose your license.

FAST FACT

An average of thirty people end their lives using physician-assisted suicide in Oregon each year.

In his efforts to undo Oregon, which were firmly rejected last week [May 26, 2004] by a federal appeals court, this was what [former] Attorney General John Ashcroft wanted to happen. Another result was likely, though: Wary of prosecution, physicians would inevitably cut back on pain medication, in fear of accidental deaths.

Physicians in Oregon who wish to participate in helping a patient die may only write out a prescription. They can be present during the death, but they must not assist the patient directly or in any way administer a deadly dose of anything.

Assisted Suicide Offers Peace of Mind

The Ashcroft court defeat comes at a dramatic moment for those of us in the movement. The 10th anniversary of the Oregon law is approaching. There have been some surprises. Probably the biggest is how few people have taken advantage of the law—only about 30 a year. That might cause some to question whether the fight is worth it, not only to keep physician-assisted suicide legal in Oregon but to get it going in other states, which proponents are trying, unsuccessfully so far, to do.

It is worth it for a simple reason: peace of mind. Studies show it is suffering that most dying people fear, not death. That means those who happen to live in Oregon, sick or not, have a kind of insurance the rest of us don't: They know they can get out of life when they are desperate to do so.

An End to Fear

I saw firsthand what happens when fear is quieted. When my mother finally had in her possession a lethal dose of Nembutal, a calm came over her that was almost weird. My aunt, who didn't know her sister was plotting to die, wondered if she might be recovering. "Your mother seems so—well," she said to me. "Can she be getting better?"

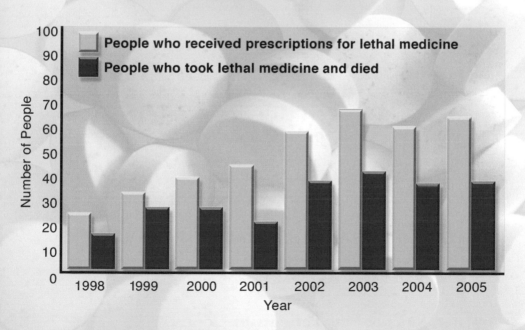

Does Physician-Assisted Suicide Offer Peace of Mind?

Though many people request prescriptions under Oregon's Death with Dignity Act, not all end up taking the lethal medication. They report just having the prescription available to them offers them peace of mind.

People who received prescriptions for lethal medicine
People who took lethal medicine and died

Source: Eighth Annual Report on Oregon's Death with Dignity Act, March 9, 2006.

Diane Pretty (left) died after being denied access to physician-assisted suicide. Pretty would have preferred to have control over her death.

In a way, I could have replied, yes, because with her fear gone, she became herself. I could tell because she started bossing me around again. "Look in my closet," she commanded. "There's an awful hat I bought in Bloomingdale's. Don't forget to return it. The receipt is in the bag."

Not in the slightest was my mother getting better physically. She had pain medication, but her nausea was almost constant, her discomfort great—in a word, she was miserable and, at the most, had only a few months, maybe weeks, to live. But she had become emotionally well because she'd returned to a place she had grown accustomed to: the driver's seat.

Assisted Suicide Puts Patients in Control

A couple of years ago, I visited some people in Oregon who had requested the means to die. Two are particularly memorable. Richard

Holmes, bearded, scruffy and 73, who lived outside of Portland, had been suffering with colon cancer—now metastasized to the liver—for about three years. Weak as he was, he could still walk and was as feisty, his son said, as he'd always been. A girlie magazine sat on his coffee table, a framed photograph of his hospice nurse on the mantle. In a small bottle in his basement, he had more than enough Nembutal to kill him.

"When I get sick enough, I'll take it," he said. "Hell, it makes sense to me. I don't want to die in a coma and not know what's going on."

And there was Laura Meirndorf from Scotts Mills, Ore., population 300. Laura, 76, who had been a logger, was a big woman with narrow eyes and swollen ankles and feet. After smoking three packs of cigarettes a day for most of her adult life, Laura got lung cancer. She decided chemo wasn't for her.

"I didn't see any point in it," she growled cheerfully. "I seen too many people go through that and then die." When she heard about the assisted-suicide law, she liked what she heard. "My kids watched their father die inch by inch. I didn't want that."

Laura's Nembutal sat on top of her refrigerator. "If I get hurtin' real bad, I can run in there and drink it down," she said with a snort. "I mean, you don't have to use it, but if you want it, it's there."

Exactly.

EVALUATING THE AUTHORS' ARGUMENTS:

In the viewpoint you just read, the author recounts the true stories of three terminally ill people who chose to have control over their own deaths. Did you find this technique effective? After reading the article, explain whether or not you agree that physician-assisted suicide should be legal, and why.

Physician-Assisted Suicide Should Not Be Legal

Frank Boehm

"Physician-assisted suicide is . . . fundamentally incompatible with the physician's role as healer."

In the following viewpoint Frank Boehm argues that physician-assisted suicide (PAS) should not be legal. Drawing on his own experience as a physician, Boehm warns that allowing doctors to kill their patients violates the fundamental doctor-patient relationship. Boehm believes that PAS is fraught with risks and complications. These include conflicts of interest between treating illness and the cost of medical care, abuse of PAS by a patient's family, and a changing cultural perception of suicide. Boehm concludes that doctors should focus on making their patients' lives more comfortable and less painful instead of helping them die.

Boehm is the author of numerous scientific publications, as well as the book *Doctors Cry Too: Essays from the Heart of a Physician.* Boehm teaches in the Vanderbilt University School of Medicine.

AS YOU READ, CONSIDER THE FOLLOWING QUESTIONS:

1. According to the author, how would society's perception of suicide change if physician-assisted suicide were legal?
2. What does the author suggest that the United States should learn from the Netherlands' experience with physician-assisted suicide?
3. Why does the author worry that PAS will eliminate expensive and risky medical treatment?

Although polls reveal that 75% of Americans believe physicians should be allowed to help end the lives of terminally ill patients at the patient's request, I fear most Americans do not understand what could actually happen if physician-assisted suicide becomes the law of the land. The American Medical Association has voted overwhelmingly to oppose physician-assisted suicide, and I wholeheartedly agree with their position.

Thousands of years of medical and moral tradition claiming that suicide is immoral and wrong and culminating with laws forbidding

Copyright © Mike Lester. Reproduced by permission of Cagle Cartoons, Inc.

physician-assisted suicide is in danger of being overturned because of a few compelling cases. It should be remembered, however, that tough cases usually make bad laws.

The Value of Life Will Diminish

Legalizing physician-assisted suicide will change the way our society thinks about suicide. We will think of it [as] moral rather than immoral, humane rather than inhumane, and legal rather than illegal. Legalizing physician-assisted suicide will also change how physicians view life and may, because of cost-cutting demands of managed care, place doctors in a conflict of interest situation. Why bother with expensive, painful, and often limited successful medical treatment when a legal, easy, less-expensive option of suicide is available?

FAST FACT

Physician-assisted suicide is legal in only four places in the whole world: the state of Oregon, Switzerland, the Netherlands, and Belgium.

Supporters of physician-assisted suicide cite the Netherlands as an example of where legalizing physician-assisted suicide is working. In my opinion, it is not. Dutch physicians participate in approximately 3600 assisted suicides each year. Reports from the Netherlands note that six out of ten Dutch physicians do not even report cases of assisted suicide.

Herbert Hendin, Executive Director of the American Suicide Foundation, was quoted in the *New York Times*: "The Netherlands has moved from assisted suicide to euthanasia, from euthanasia for people who are terminally ill to euthanasia for those who are chronically ill, from euthanasia for physical illness to euthanasia for psychological distress, and from voluntary euthanasia to involuntary euthanasia."

The Netherlands' experience has shown us that thousands of physician-assisted suicides are undertaken because of family request, not the patient. Physician-assisted suicide cannot be adequately controlled and therefore should not become legal in America.

A Doctor's Job Is to Save Lives

We need to encourage physicians to assist patients in making the end of their lives easier and less painful. We have the tools; we just need

Some believe that physician-assisted suicide is incompatible with a doctor's role to heal people.

the will. Studies show that physicians already help patients die peacefully without pain and with dignity, yet we must teach all of our practitioners that it is permissible, even mandatory, to properly treat pain and discomfort. Once pain relief has been achieved, most patients requesting physician-assisted suicide relent.

Linda Emmanuel, American Medical Association Vice-President for Ethical Standards and Director of its Institute for Ethics, was quoted: "This is a defining moment in medicine. If doctors are allowed to kill patients, the doctor-patient relationship will never be the same again. If killing patients is an option, how can I expect you to trust me to do all I can to help you? Who will regulate what doctors do? How will we view the old and sick, the patients with Alzheimer's and chronic debilitating diseases whose medical expenses are piling up, thereby taking precious healthcare dollars from the system and the family as well? Will families be able to agree and for what reason will they agree?"

Assisted Suicide Is Anti-American

The late Supreme Court Justice [William] Rehnquist in a ruling on physician-assisted suicide stated that "Physician-assisted suicide goes counter to American history, tradition, laws, and moral values. It is fundamentally incompatible with the physician's role as healer."

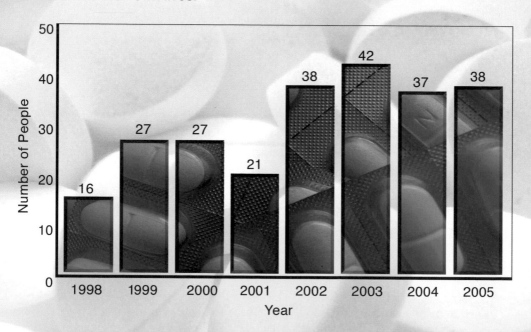

Physician-Assisted Suicide Since 1998

As of 2005, a total of 246 people had elected to enact Oregon's Assisted Suicide Law and end their own lives.

Source: International Task Force on Euthanasia and Assisted Suicide.

I also agree with what Michael J. Sandel, a political philosophy teacher at Harvard, said about the subject: "Physician-assisted suicide is one of the rare issues in which ambiguity is preferable to moral consistency in which judgments on a case-by-case basis are better than strict laws or guidelines about what is right and what is wrong. Sometimes it is better just to leave things murky."

EVALUATING THE AUTHORS' ARGUMENTS:

Boehm argues that physician-assisted suicide violates the oath that doctors take requiring them to "do no harm." But the author of the previous viewpoint, Betty Rollin, argues that physicians help their terminally ill patients when they help them end their suffering. What do you think—does physician-assisted suicide help or hurt terminally ill patients? Support your answer with evidence from the text.

Physician-Assisted Suicide Threatens the Elderly and the Sick

Wesley J. Smith

"Placing... approval on some suicides would send an insidious message to dying patients that they are burdens; that their illness does make them less worthy of being loved."

In the following viewpoint Wesley J. Smith argues that legalizing euthanasia would pose a serious risk to elderly and sick patients. He explains that legalizing euthanasia would send the message that some lives are worth neither living nor improving with medical care. Physician-assisted suicide could also lead to the abuse of old and sick people—Smith warns that some patients may actually have longer to live than their diagnosis leads them to believe. Furthermore, enterprising relatives could convince their elders to receive assisted suicide in order to force an early inheritance or to save money on prolonged medical care. Finally, Smith cautions that legalizing euthanasia for one group of people will inevitably lead to euthanasia being performed on other groups of people,

Wesley J. Smith, "Assisting Suicides Is Bad Law, Policy: Sacramento Is Considering Creating an Oregon-Style System to End Lives," The Center for People with Disabilities, www.cpwd-ilc.org, October 25, 2005. Reproduced by permission of the author.

such as the disabled, the depressed, and undesirable children.

Smith is a lawyer for the International Task Force on Euthanasia and Assisted Suicide.

AS YOU READ, CONSIDER THE FOLLOWING QUESTIONS:
1. What does the word "euphemism" mean in the context of the viewpoint?
2. What evidence does the author give that Oregon's euthanasia laws are being abused?
3. What does the author say that people who are dying need?

Advocates of assisted suicide label hastened death a "compassionate choice." But such gooey euphemisms seek to hide the harsh truth: Assisted suicide isn't about caring: It is about the intentional ending of human life—an act barred by the Hippocratic Oath for more than 2000 years.

We are told that assisted suicide would be restricted to cases of unbearable suffering. Yet, legislation in California to legalize assisted suicide—AB651 by Assemblywoman Patty Berg, D-Eureka—contains no such requirement. Nor does the law in Oregon, where doctors who assist suicides report that most patients do not seek death because of pain, but because they can no longer engage in enjoyable activities, fear losing dignity or are worried about becoming burdens.

> **FAST FACT**
>
> A 1996 study of more than eight hundred critical-care nurses shows that 20 percent admitted to hastening the death of a terminally ill patient.

The Wrong Message

Don't get me wrong: These are important issues that cry out for proper care. Thankfully, we have hospice—true death with dignity—to treat these needs. Indeed, studies show that when these problems are addressed, suicidal desires almost always disappear.

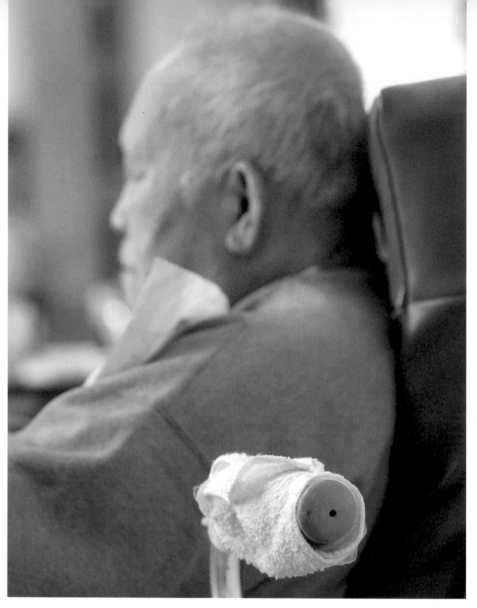

Physician-assisted suicide could threaten one of America's most vulnerable populations, the elderly.

While acknowledging the truth of the previous sentence, assisted-suicide proponents contend there will always be a few people who want assisted suicide, anyway. But placing California's seal of approval on some suicides would send an insidious message to dying patients that they are burdens; that their illness does make them less worthy of being loved; that they will die in agony. And it would signal the broader society, including young people, that suicide is right in some cases.

The Slippery Slope—Many Will Be Murdered

Legalizing assisted suicide would also be very risky. The Netherlands proves that when mercy killing is allowed for the few, it steadily spreads. In the past 30 years, Dutch doctors have gone from killing the terminally ill, to the disabled, and even to the depressed who aren't physically sick. Recent headlines report that infanticide of dying and disabled babies will soon be legalized by the Dutch Parliament.

Assisted-suicide boosters claim it would be different here and point to Oregon to show that there is no "slippery slope." But nobody knows what is actually going on in Oregon. The state conducts no independent

"Hmm, if I may, Mrs Hamilton, before we discuss assisted suicide, I do feel I should at least examine your husband"

There is concern that physician-assisted suicide could lead to the murder of the elderly to avoid expensive medical bills.

reviews of assisted suicide, for example, to ensure that only dying patients receive lethal prescriptions. Moreover, almost all the published data about Oregon cited by advocates are based primarily on information provided by death-prescribing doctors—who are as likely to report violating the law as they are to tell the IRS that they cheated on their taxes.

The Potential for Abuse
Still, abuses have been revealed. In the only case in which the medical records of a potential assisted suicide were independently reviewed, a peer-reviewed report in the *Journal of the American Psychiatric Association* disclosed that the patient received a lethal prescription almost

two years before he died naturally. Yet, Oregon law requires that the patient be likely to die within 6 months. Not only that, but the patient was permitted to keep his pills even after being hospitalized as delusional. In another case reported in the *Oregonian*, a woman with Alzheimer's disease and cancer received assisted suicide even after a psychiatrist reported that she didn't know what she was asking for and that her daughter was the driving force behind the request.

We must also take heed of the real world in which assisted suicide would exist. California health services for the poor are being cut to the bone. The number of medically uninsured Californians exceeds the entire population of Oregon, and many people with insurance are in HMOs, which make profits by limiting costs. The drugs used in an assisted suicide would cost less than $100. Yet, it could cost $100,000 to provide quality care so the patient doesn't want suicide.

Help the Dying, Don't Hurt Them

Then, there are issues of inheritance and life insurance. Elder abuse and neglect are terrible concerns. These and other problems make assisted suicide especially dangerous.

People who are dying need love, inclusion, and medical care that values their lives, not hastens their deaths. Legalizing assisted suicide in California would be bad medicine and even worse public policy.

EVALUATING THE AUTHORS' ARGUMENTS:

In this viewpoint Smith argues that legalizing assisted suicide puts elderly and sick people at risk for abuse. If assisted suicide were to become legal in your state, what sorts of safeguards would you suggest in order to prevent the old and sick from being taken advantage of? In your opinion, is it possible to prevent such abuse through safeguards, or will any form of legalized assisted suicide be prone to abuse? Explain your answer.

Physician-Assisted Suicide Does Not Threaten the Elderly and the Sick

"If we are to have free will, that free will should include not only how we live our lives, but how long we live them."

Keith Taylor

In the following viewpoint Keith Taylor argues that physician-assisted suicide helps sick and elderly people choose when and how they die. He discusses the case of his friend Freddie, who slowly died from cancer. Because Freddie did not have the option of electing physician-assisted suicide, he and his family were forced to endure weeks of misery before he finally died. Had Freddie been able to choose the timing of his death, the author contends, he and his family would have been spared horrible suffering. Taylor concludes that Freddie and those like him should be free to make intensely personal decisions such as when to end their own lives. The government, Taylor believes, has no right to interfere in such matters by refusing people the opportunity to control their deaths.

Taylor is a retired naval officer and a columnist for a national weekly newspaper.

Keith Taylor, "Was Dr. Kevorkian Right? Why Cling to a Life Without Savor?" *Free Inquiry*, vol. 23, Spring 2003, pp. 29–30. Copyright 2003 Council for Democratic and Secular Humanism, Inc. Reproduced by permission.

AS YOU READ, CONSIDER THE FOLLOWING QUESTIONS:
1. The author begins his essay by explaining his belief that elderly people make important contributions to society. Why, then, does he ultimately support legalized assisted suicide?
2. Why did Freddie turn down the opportunity to undergo chemotherapy, as reported by the author?
3. What does the word "septuagenarian" mean in the context of the viewpoint?

After twenty-three years in the Navy and another twenty-two as an insurance broker, I can do what I choose. That mostly involves work of some sort, but work I enjoy. I did standup comedy for a few years, but quit because I was funnier than the audience realized. I also taught defensive driving to folks who had received tickets. Surely it wasn't a coincidence that a decrease in traffic deaths coincided with my teaching. Now I'm a columnist for a national weekly newspaper and make it into print elsewhere often. My

Some of America's elderly view physician-assisted suicide laws as a dignified way to comfortably end their lives when the time is right.

research for recent articles has included running a marathon and hiking up the highest mountain in California.

I'm not alone in my enthusiasm. One friend, age eighty-eight, has been a journalist, a television and radio newsman, and a politician. Today, he is a syndicated columnist, a freelance writer, and is one of the first people television interviewers head for when there's a political question to be put into perspective. Another friend, mid-seventies, is a leading scientist, runs an international research institute, teaches regularly in France and Japan in the native languages, and is up to his ears in projects. The list is extensive. Six years ago, a group, mostly gray-haired people, founded an organization dedicated to rational thought and to reason. Today that group, now with many young people, is alive and well. Folks of all ages are sharing ideas. Everybody is learning from each other.

Why then would I suggest that Dr. [Jack] Kevorkian [who illegally assisted nearly 100 people to die] is on the right track? Isn't he the one who tries to shorten lives?

A Good Life Matters More than a Long Life

I postulate that living is not merely breathing. It's not living as we know it when the ability to communicate is no longer with us, when the love of those close to us has turned to pity, and when waking up simply means another day to be lived in pain.

We who have been making hard decisions for so many years must have the right to make that final decision, the hardest one of all. Sometime back I wrote the following for the *Los Angeles Times*: An old friend back in Indiana is now at the point where a needle in one arm provides the sustenance to keep him breathing and one in the other arm gives him the morphine to keep him asleep. He's been like that for more than a week. When I talk to his other friends in Indiana we often slip and refer to him in the past tense.

It's been a painful few weeks. Less than a month ago I made my last call from San Diego to Ft. Wayne to talk to Freddie. It was one of several dozen conversations we shared over the past year. The first call was made because Trudy, his wife, asked me. "Keith could you call Freddie? He has just been diagnosed with cancer and really needs someone to cheer him up."

Who Has Used Physician-Assisted Suicide?

The 246 people who have used Oregon's assisted suicide law to end their lives were the following gender, age, and race:

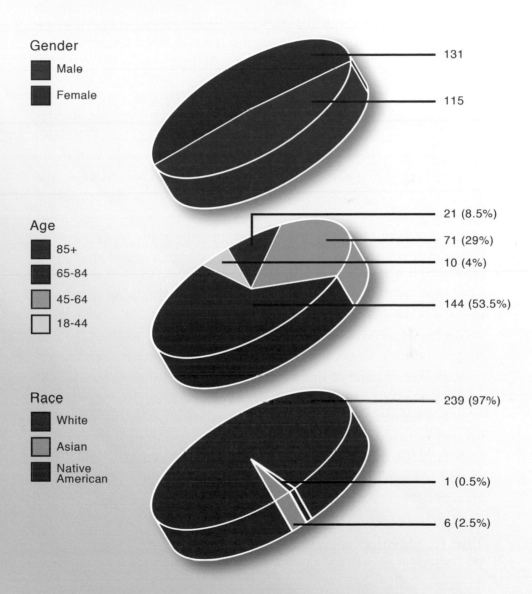

Gender
- Male
- Female

131
115

Age
- 85+
- 65-84
- 45-64
- 18-44

21 (8.5%)
71 (29%)
10 (4%)
144 (53.5%)

Race
- White
- Asian
- Native American

239 (97%)
1 (0.5%)
6 (2.5%)

Source: Eighth Annual Report on Oregon's Death with Dignity Act, March 9, 2006.

Wow! Talk about a rough assignment. I didn't want to make that call, but Freddie had been my friend for fifty-five years, and I couldn't refuse. Happily, it turned out to be a piece of cake. We chatted about his illness. Then he remembered something funny we'd done and we laughed about it. The banter continued and, sure enough, I cheered him up just like Trudy asked. Better yet, he cheered me up. Friends do that. We had so many wonderful memories that maudlin thoughts were crowded out of our minds.

Death Can Just Be Delayed, Never Stopped

Freddie was ill, no doubt about it. The doctors removed his bladder. That didn't do it. He still had cancer in his lymph glands. The only option left was chemotherapy. That wouldn't do. Freddie had seen a friend suffer horribly from the stuff. My old friend turned down this slim chance to gain a few months, perhaps a year, at the cost of excruciating pain.

So far as I could tell, he made the right choice. He was always upbeat and he managed to avoid slipping into despair like so many people facing death. He made a trip to Florida, a few excursions up to a gambling boat on Lake Michigan, and was even talking of coming west for one more get-together.

Neither of us pussyfooted around the subject. He still had the cancer and nothing was going to stop it—nothing except a heart attack perhaps. He had one of them too, a big one. Fortunately he was with a friend who also had heart disease and carried nitroglycerin. He gave a pill to Freddie and my friend lived to await the ravages of the cancer.

Later he told a mutual friend, "I wish that had done it for me. You know I didn't miss a thing in this old life. If I had it to do all over again I wouldn't have changed a bit of it. I just don't want to finish up a pathetic sick old man."

The Ill Should Not Be Made to Suffer

Yet, that's what he is doing. He spent something like three weeks in the hospital, the last week unconscious in intensive care. I called Trudy and tried to tell her, "If he wakes up, tell him I called." Septuagenarian men aren't supposed to cry but I didn't make it. Trudy cried along with me and said, "I will."

Being allowed to take control of their death is a comfort to many terminally ill patients.

Both of us were sure he wouldn't wake up, but I needed to say something. Everybody I talk to now is concerned for Trudy and the hell she's going through with her husband of thirty years now merely a diapered breathing body far removed from her world. We wonder how much money she'll have left after paying all the bills.

He's home and still unconscious. If they discontinue the morphine he'll wake up and scream until he dies. Or, they can sever a nerve and he might wake up without pain but he'd know he was paralyzed.

Despite all the flowery words on pretty get-well cards, and the high flown religious sentiments, death seldom is dignified. Doctor Kevorkian has the answer. We will just have to recognize it.

The Elderly Deserve to Control Their Own Lives

My article was pure emotion, a catharsis. My friend had been one of the happiest guys I ever knew. He deserved much more than this in his final days. Mercifully, Freddie died even before the article ran in the paper.

Then the letters rolled in, most of them from folks about my age. A few claimed I was playing God and only God could take a life. Most felt that we should be in control of our own lives, even to the extent of being able to end them if we wished.

I insist that if we are to have free will, that free will should include not only how we live our lives, but how long we live them. The government's only role is to butt out.

EVALUATING THE AUTHORS' ARGUMENTS:

In this viewpoint Taylor argues that assisted suicide would benefit sick and elderly patients by giving them control over the quality of their lives. Do you think it is more important to have a high quality of life, or to be alive for as long as possible? Support your answer using evidence from the texts you have read.

Physician-Assisted Suicide Threatens the Severely Handicapped

"Our efforts should focus on making our communities more responsive to those who need help to live, rather than figuring out these policies to help people die."

Richard Radtke

In the following viewpoint Richard Radtke argues that legalizing physician-assisted suicide would threaten severely handicapped people. He begins by discussing his own experience with disability after contracting a severe form of multiple sclerosis (MS). In the first two years of his illness, Radtke was so depressed that he would have sought suicide if the option had been available. Had he killed himself, however, Radtke believes he would have missed the rich and meaningful life he has since lived. He stresses that the depression faced by newly disabled people often passes and that disabled people end up more satisfied with their lives than other people. He concludes that disabled people face many new forms of stress, including their fear of becoming a burden to their

Richard Radtke, "A Case Against Physician-Assisted Suicide," *Journal of Disability Policy Studies*, vol. 16, Summer 2005, pp. 58–60. Copyright 2005 Pro-Ed. Reproduced by permission.

caretakers and their struggle to come to terms with their new lives. Society should devote its resources to helping disabled people deal with these difficulties, not to passing policies that seek to end their lives.

Radtke is the president and CEO of the Sea of Dreams Foundation, a nonprofit organization founded to provide disadvantaged people with opportunities to achieve their full potential.

AS YOU READ, CONSIDER THE FOLLOWING QUESTIONS:
1. Name three professional accomplishments of Radtke's since he became disabled.
2. What does the word "naivete" mean in the context of the viewpoint?
3. How does the author respond to the argument that assisted suicide helps those who are in great pain?

The discussion about physician-assisted suicide often centers on the issues of unbearable pain and dignity. Issues are often wrought with attitude bias, clouded perceptions, and fear. Most individuals when asked whether they or others should suffer unbearable pain and an undignified demise would state a resounding "no". No one wants anyone to suffer, and everyone deserves dignity. However, let us not allow the arguments on assisted suicide [to] cloud the major issues of better pain management, palliative care and hospice, and an increased quality of life, which would make this issue a moot point. We need to work toward better life, not toward ways to end it.

I Was Supposed to Die

Lest you think my convictions are based on a foundation of naivete and self delusion, I will use myself and the experiences of my life as a case study.

My condition is incurable. My original prognosis was that I would be dead 5 years ago [by the year 2000], from the rapid progression of my disease. I have lost many bodily functions. I cannot move from the neck down. For the entire first 2 years of my disability, I have to admit, I was very depressed. I had to ask people for help where I never

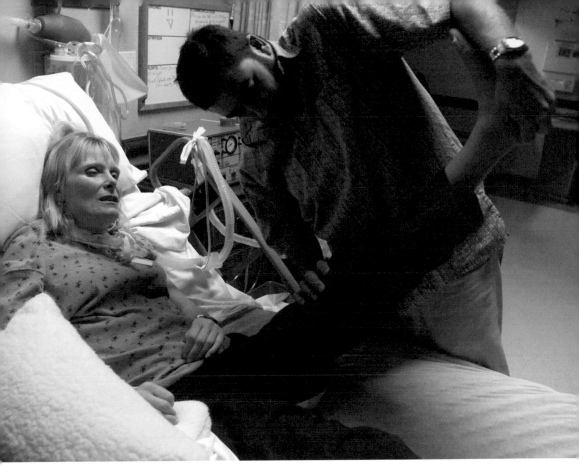

Opponents of physician-assisted suicide claim the practice reduces the focus on rehabilitation and care of disabled people.

had to ask for help before. During that darkest period, I thought about suicide. If procedures were available to help me end my life, I might well be dead now. I still think physician-assisted suicide is wrong.

The Newly Disabled Are Frequently Depressed and Vulnerable

People with illness and disability are statistically more likely to have feelings of suicide, especially in the early period after the onset of a significant disability because of psychosocial issues, such as feeling like a burden on family and fears about future loss of function associated with increases in disability. However, research overwhelmingly shows that after an adjustment period, people with disabilities rate their own quality of life as high or higher than the general public.

People with disabilities are very familiar with these issues. . . .

Going through any type of disability takes mental, emotional, and social support: There should be counseling to support self-esteem, there should be employment support and transportation support, looking at what options may be possible. People who have disabilities must be able to reach out and feel that they are part of the world. When you

Disabled people passionately reject the suggestion that their lives are not worth living.

are closed in, your whole world becomes smaller and smaller. You feel that there are few options left.

Let us look at autonomy. I have to ask people for help for everything from putting on my headset for my computer to helping me eat to the one people have the most fear about—going to the bathroom. That is part of my life; and, after a while, it's become just life. We all do things that, if you stopped and pondered them, you might say, "Maybe I don't want to do these things, but I can't stop them." You can't stop going to the bathroom, you can't stop eating. When I was depressed, I considered cutting my losses by "checking out." I did not see how I could maintain my sense of autonomy if I was so reliant on help.

Disabled Lives Can Be Meaningful

Now, let's look at what I'm doing today. I spent 20 years as a research professor at the University of Hawaii. I've published more than 70 papers. I'm considered an expert in my field. I retired from the university in July. I'm now the president and CEO of the Sea of Dreams Foundation, which is a full-time organization set up to assist people with disabilities. We have a camp for youth with disabilities to support activities that build their self-esteem. All those things could have been lost 20 years ago if I had someone to help me commit suicide. . . .

Some people may challenge my position against assisted suicide, pointing out that I had advanced education, resources, or personal strengths that others may not have to face a life with a disability. My answer is that we must find ways to give these supports to others, as it may make a life-

and-death difference. You don't need a PhD to get through severe losses in your life. I have seen people go through terrible times in the small community where I grew up in Indiana. There is a resiliency in that community that gets them through. I don't know whether I consider myself a particularly strong person. I do consider myself focused,

Many disabled people, such as this quadriplegic, have found alternative ways to continue to work and pursue their hobbies.

but being focused or having inner strength are qualities that people can acquire.

I have also heard the argument that assisted suicide must be available for individuals with unmanageable pain. I suffer from trigeminal neuralgia, an inflammation of one of the nerves in my face. This goes along with my MS and has been described as the worst pain known to man. The pain does not even respond to morphine, so I take a whole series of medications. There are more options available through medicine today than ever before to make life more comfortable. Let us spend our time, money, and effort working on pain management rather than on ways to hasten death. . . .

The Disabled Need Help to Live, Not Die

Everyone encountering a disability should have resources addressing their spiritual life, emotional life, financial life, and medical life to help with the problems and fears that they experience. There is a big fear of being a burden on family finances, society, the world. Feeling like a burden on your family and friends is devastating: Nobody wants to be a burden. There is so much fear in our society of having a disability and needing help. Let us deal with the fear rather than resorting to assisted suicide. We can work on programs that offer respite for caregivers. Our efforts should focus on making our communities more responsive to those who need help to live, rather than figuring out these policies to help people die. . . .

Other points to consider are individual free choice (it is easy to have coercion under duress), the length of life (it is difficult for anyone to predict how long someone will live; medical science is an inaccurate art that changes daily), quality of life (whose scale do we use?), and the prospect for harsher application of assisted suicide (once one group is subjected, it is easier to open it to other groups). Feelings of duress because of financial and care-taking concerns repress "free choice" and cloud our perceptions of quality of life. In the absence of any real choice and in the face of duress, death by assisted suicide becomes not an act of personal autonomy but an act of desperation. Furthermore, once we accept suicide as "therapy" we become more accepting of its "applications" to other groups. This would be an insidious breach of our approach to living and dying.

EVALUATING THE AUTHORS' ARGUMENTS:

In the viewpoint you just read, Richard Radtke draws on personal experience to make his argument against physician-assisted suicide. How were your ideas about assisted suicide changed after reading this firsthand experience? What writing techniques did Radtke use that someone who is not disabled would be unable to employ?

Physician-Assisted Suicide Offers Options to the Severely Handicapped

Joan Ryan

"It's demeaning to say disabled people don't have the capacity or the right to make the choices others do."

In the following viewpoint Joan Ryan rebuts disability-rights groups who claim that assisted suicide threatens the handicapped. In response to concerns that assisted suicide could be used to kill off the disabled, Ryan cites statistics from Oregon's Death with Dignity Act to show that such fears about legalized assisted suicide have not come true. For example, she points out that no person suffering from a fixed disability, that is, a disability not caused by a terminal illness, has ever taken advantage of assisted suicide. Moreover, she argues, Oregon's law has strict safeguards in place to prevent others from encouraging a person to commit suicide against their will. She concludes that assisted suicide does not threaten the disabled but instead offers them the ability to be in control of their lives and deaths.

Ryan is a columnist for the *San Francisco Chronicle*, from which this viewpoint is taken.

AS YOU READ, CONSIDER THE FOLLOWING QUESTIONS:
1. What does the word "palliative" mean in the context of the viewpoint?
2. According to the author, what is a person in Oregon required to do before they can be be eligible for physician assisted suicide?
3. According to the author, how does keeping assisted suicide illegal hurt terminally ill patients and their families?

All things being equal, I will always root for more options rather than fewer. I appreciate a government that gives me the freedom to make my own decisions: where I go to school, what jobs I take, where I live, how many children I have, when and whether to marry.

California's contemplation of physician-assisted suicide laws has been met with much controversy and protest.

I imagine most Americans are with me on this one. We want our government to let us live as we choose. So why do we stand for a government that won't let us die as we choose?

Two state legislators plan to introduce a bill this year that would make physician-assisted suicide legal in California. The bill will be modeled on the law in Oregon, the only state in which assisted suicide is legal. The law applies only to terminally ill patients with less than six months to live.

To acquire the medication necessary to bring on death, a person must get the approval of two doctors who determine that the person is mentally competent. If the physicians suspect depression, they can compel a psychiatric evaluation. The person must then make a written and oral request. After a waiting period, the doctor can write the prescription. The process generally takes about two weeks. Patients must be capable of administering the dosage themselves.

Disability-Rights Groups Are Wary

Aside from religious objections, the strongest arguments against the Oregon law—as now against the proposed California one—have come from disability-rights groups. Their concerns are understandable.

"Lives of people with disabilities have historically not been valued, and any person affected by this bill is de facto a person of disability," said Deborah Doctor of Protection & Advocacy Inc., a California group that has not taken a position on the proposal yet. "It opens the door to further devaluation of the lives of people with disabilities."

Stephen Drake is a research analyst for Not Dead Yet, a disability-rights group based in Illinois that is mounting opposition to California's bill. He says the proposal, like Oregon's law, discriminates against the disabled. It makes suicide legal and accessible to them but not for others, in effect clearing the way for the disabled to kill themselves.

"In California and every other state, health care workers and law enforcement professionals are supposed to respond to those who want to commit suicide and stop them," Drake said. "But by allowing this one group to carry out suicide with assistance says it is less valuable than everyone else is. This is a door opener to the larger movement of euthanasia."

Not All Disabilities Are Equal

He said he fears families, doctors and health maintenance organizations would be given the means to end the lives of vulnerable disabled people who are considered a costly burden.

But doctors who treat dying patients see a great difference between those who have a fixed disability and those who have become disabled

Opponents of physician-assisted suicide believe attempts should be made to make the elderly and sick more comfortable instead of ending their lives.

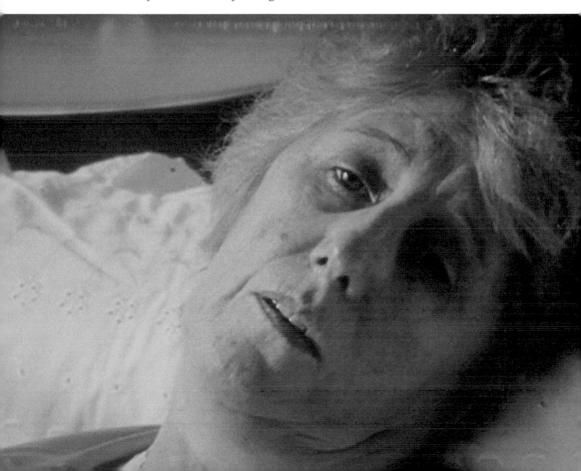

George Eighmey, executive director of Compassion in Dying, speaks about why he believes physician-assisted suicide should be legal during a 2003 conference.

through terminal illness. In the latter, the disability is progressing.

"They are clinically and morally different situations," said Dr. Robert Brody, a UCSF medical professor who is also chief of the Pain Consultation Clinic and the ethics committee at San Francisco General Hospital. He has worked with Compassion in Dying, the group that pushed for the Oregon law.

He understands why disabled people might fear such a law, given the history of abuse and even demonization. "Is a disabled person vulnerable? Perhaps, but not necessarily. I think it's demeaning to say disabled people don't have the capacity or the right to make the choices others do. How is that respecting the rights of people with disabilities?"

Fears Have Proved Unwarranted

The experience in Oregon during the past six years is instructive, especially in assessing the legitimacy of the arguments against the California proposal. None of the doomsday predictions have come true. It has not led to euthanasia, in which a doctor or family member, without the dying person's participation, hastens death. And no person with a fixed disability has been assisted in suicide. The safeguards in the law make such an act illegal.

From 1998 through 2003, just 171 people in Oregon ended their lives through physician-assisted suicide. Eighty-eight percent were 55 or older. Many who acquired the medication never used it but said they were comforted by having the option readily available. The reasons patients gave for seeking assisted suicide were similar: Most said they wanted to end their lives because they had lost their autonomy, could no longer engage in activities that made life enjoyable, and feared losing their dignity.

Many in the disabled community understandably take offense at this last reason. Many disabled people live their entire lives with such so-called indignities and still find life worth living. But shouldn't each of us decide for ourselves what makes life worth living? Should my standard be forced on you or yours on me?

Choices About Death Protect Dignity and Autonomy

"We all die," said Dr. Steven Pantilat, director of the Palliative Care Service at UCSF. He teaches a course on end-of-life care at the university. "The way we die in America is often very different from the way we want to die. We can do it better, giving people meaningful time with their families, allowing them to be at home. But most end up prisoners of technology."

Pantilat said one or two patients a year ask him to help hasten their deaths. He always asks, "Why are you bringing this up today?" He listens to their fears, and in almost every case, the requests go away when they are assured their pain can be managed and that they can be cared for with dignity.

"Good palliative care can take care of most of the fears people have about dying," he said, making note of the tiny percentage of people in Oregon who have made use of the law. Still, with safeguards in place, he supports assisted suicide for those few people who feel strongly about being in control of their deaths. In California now, such people cannot be with family and friends in those final moments; aiding and abetting a suicide is illegal.

We recognize that we have different values and live in different circumstances from each other, and we make individual decisions that reflect those variables. We don't want the government telling us how to live our lives. Why, then, do we tolerate it telling us how to end them?

EVALUATING THE AUTHORS' ARGUMENTS:

In this viewpoint Ryan argues that assisted suicide would give disabled people options, not threaten them. In the previous viewpoint Richard Radtke argues that disabled people's depression makes them vulnerable to choosing death when they otherwise would not. In your opinion, at what point can people be trusted to make the right decision about ending their lives? Should people have options about death, or should they be protected from rashly hurting themselves?

Facts About Euthanasia

Euthanasia and Physician-Assisted Suicide Around the World

- According to SAVES, the South Australian Voluntary Euthanasia Society, most countries routinely withhold burdensome or futile treatment from a dying patient, even if doing so hastens the patient's death.
- SAVES also states that many countries regularly treat the pain or suffering of dying patients with strong medicines, even if the medicines could potentially kill the patient.
- The Dutch Supreme Court voted to legalize euthanasia in 1984, provided that doctors met certain strict guidelines in carrying out the procedure.
- Dutch doctors are required by law to report all cases of assisted death or euthanasia to a medical examiner, who reports to a district attorney, who decides whether to prosecute for murder.
- According to the Nightingale Alliance, in the Netherlands 61 percent of the patients who died from lethal doses of painkillers in 1990 never discussed the decision with their doctors, despite the fact that 27 percent of the patients were competent enough to do so.
- A 2001 study of euthanasia practices conducted by the Dutch government showed that only about half of Dutch doctors faithfully report cases of euthanasia.
- Physician-assisted suicide is legal in four places—the state of Oregon, the Netherlands, Belgium, and Switzerland.
- Belgium legalized physician-assisted suicide in 2002.
- Switzerland legalized physician-assisted suicide in 1941.
- The state of Oregon legalized physician-assisted suicide in 1997.
- The Netherlands legalized physician-assisted suicide in 2002.
- Norway imposes criminal sanctions against those who assist with suicide by charging them with "accessory to murder."
- In England and Wales there is a possibility of up to fourteen years imprisonment for anybody assisting a suicide.

- Assisted suicide is a crime in the Republic of Ireland.
- In Hungary, assistance in suicide or attempted suicide is punishable by up to five years imprisonment.

Euthanasia and Physician-Assisted Suicide in the United States

- Oregon is the only state in the United States where physician-assisted suicide is legal.
- A citizens' initiative passed Oregon's Death with Dignity Act in November 1994, but a court injunction delayed action until 1997.
- Six states—Alaska, California, Hawaii, Maine, Michigan, and Washington—have either defeated laws to allow physician-assisted suicide or declared that their constitutions do not guarantee a right to physician-assisted suicide.
- In 1997 the U.S. Supreme Court declared that the federal constitution does not guarantee the right to assisted suicide.
- Dr. Jack Kevorkian, a famous euthanasia advocate and practitioner, was sentenced to ten to twenty-five years in prison for assisting in the death of Thomas Youk in 1999.
- Between 1920 and 1993, 519 cases of mercy killing were recorded in the United States, with ninety-two percent of those cases occurring since 1973.
- About one out of every five kidney dialysis patients dies from refusing further dialysis, even though they know they will most likely die within the next two weeks.
- In 1991 a grand jury refused to indict Dr. Timothy Quill on charges of assisting suicide, which could result in a five- to fifteen- year prison sentence, after he wrote a letter to the *New England Journal of Medicine* about prescribing a lethal dose of barbiturates to a patient he knew intended to kill herself.

According to the Department of Human Services, Oregon State Public Health:

- Between 1998 and the end of 2005, 246 people committed suicide under Oregon's Death with Dignity Law.
- The number of prescriptions written for lethal medications has

steadily climbed every year since 1998, with sixty-four prescriptions written in 2005.

- Of the sixty-four people who were prescribed lethal medications in 2005, half either died of their illness before they committed suicide or were still alive at the end of the year.
- The majority of people who choose assisted suicide are college-educated, white, married men who suffer from terminal cancer.
- The top five reasons given by patients who elected physician-assisted suicide in 2005 were:
  1. Fear of decreasing ability to do enjoyable activities
  2. Fear of loss of dignity
  3. Fear of losing autonomy
  4. Fear of losing control of bodily functions
  5. Fear of being a burden

Public Opinion About Euthanasia and Physician-Assisted Suicide

According to a survey conducted in November 2005 by the Pew Research Center for People and the Press:

- The vast majority of Americans approve of laws that give patients the right to die when they choose.
- Just 22 percent of Americans believe that doctors and nurses should always do everything they can to save a life, while 70 percent say there are situations in which a patient should be allowed to die.
- In cases where terminally ill patients cannot communicate their own wishes, about three quarters (74 percent) of Americans believe that family members have the right to decide whether to discontinue medical treatment on the patient's behalf.
- Eighty four percent of Americans approve of laws recognizing the right of terminally ill patients to decide whether to allow medical treatment to keep them alive, while just 10 percent disapprove of such laws.
- The nation is divided over whether to legalize physician-assisted suicide. Just 46 percent of Americans approve of such laws, while 45 percent disapprove. The remaining 9 percent are undecided.

A May 2006 Gallup poll found that

- 75 percent of Americans support "allowing a doctor to take the life of a patient who is suffering from an incurable disease and wants to die."
- People most likely to oppose euthanasia were frequent church-goers, senior citizens, conservatives, Republicans, African Americans, or had low levels of education.

Glossary

active euthanasia: A form of euthanasia in which actions are taken to purposefully cause the death of an individual.

autonomy: A person's right or ability to act on behalf of his or her own interests without the permission or assistance of others.

Death with Dignity Act: The Oregon law originally passed in November 1994 that legalized physician-assisted suicide. Facing repeated legal challenges, the law finally went into action in 1997.

eugenic: Relating to eugenics, which is the study of how to improve the human race by restricting reproduction to those people who have certain desirable qualities.

euthanasia: From the Greek for "good death," the intentional ending of a human life either by giving the person lethal drugs or by purposefully withholding life-saving treatment.

Hippocratic oath: Named for Hippocrates of Cos, an ancient Greek physician who is regarded as the father of medicine, this was a pledge taken by all doctors in ancient Greece to observe certain regulations and moral guidelines. Since then, upon graduating from medical school, doctors typically take some variation of the oath.

hospice: A program designed for terminally ill patients that provides care for their emotional, spiritual, social, and financial needs. Such programs either provide a place for patients to live or care for patients in their own homes.

involuntary euthanasia: A form of euthanasia in which an individual who is unable to communicate, or who has not actively pursued the means to die, is nevertheless made to die, either through active or passive means.

life support: Prolonged medical care without which a patient will die, such as respirators to breathe for them or feeding tubes to provide nourishment.

palliative care: Medical care designed to relieve or lessen the symptoms of a disease, such as the pain or suffering associated with it. Palliative care does not treat the disease itself.

PAS: See **physician-assisted suicide**.

passive euthanasia: Also referred to as "allowing to die," a form of euthanasia in which life-saving treatment is withheld for the purpose of letting a terminally ill, incurable, or PVS patient die.

persistent vegetative state: Also referred to as a "vegetative state," a medical condition in which patients are unconscious, nonresponsive, and living with diminished brain function. Patients in such a condition rarely improve, though with feeding tubes and hydration they may be kept alive indefinitely.

physician-assisted suicide: Also referred to as "assisted suicide," this practice involves a doctor prescribing lethal doses of medication to terminally ill patients who have requested help with dying.

PVS: See **persistent vegetative state**.

voluntary euthanasia: A form of euthanasia in which an individual who is of sound mind and able to communicate actively requests and pursues the means to die.

Organizations to Contact

American Civil Liberties Union (ACLU)
125 Broad St., 18th Floor
New York, NY 10004
Web site: www.aclu.org

The ACLU champions the rights of individuals in right-to-die and euthanasia cases as well as in many other civil rights issues. The ACLU Foundation provides legal defense, research, and education. The organization publishes the quarterly *Civil Liberties* and various pamphlets, books, and position papers.

The American Life League (ALL)
PO Box 1350
Stafford, VA 22555
(540) 659-4171
Web site: www.all.org

The league believes that human life is sacred. It works to educate Americans about the dangers of all forms of euthanasia and opposes legislative efforts that would legalize or increase its incidence. It publishes the bimonthly pro-life magazine *Celebrate Life* and distributes videos, brochures, and newsletters monitoring euthanasia-related developments.

American Society of Law, Medicine, and Ethics
765 Commonwealth Ave., Suite 1634
Boston, MA 02215
(617) 262-4990
e-mail: info@aslme.org
Web site: www.aslme.org

The society's members include physicians, attorneys, health care administrators, and others interested in the relationship between law, medicine, and ethics. The organization has an information clearinghouse and a library, and it acts as a forum for discussion of issues such as euthanasia and assisted suicide.

Autonomy, Inc.
14 Strawberry Hill Ln.
Danvers, MA 01923
(617) 320-0506
e-mail: info@autonomynow.org
Web site: www.autonomynow.org

Autonomy, Inc. represents the interests of disabled people who want legal, safe access to physician-assisted dying (PAD) in matters of pain management, hospice care, and legalizing PAD. The organization also supports Oregon's Death with Dignity Act and files amicus curiae briefs in major "right-to-die" cases. Through their Web site, Autonomy offers articles and an extensive bibliography of readings about handicapped people and euthanasia.

Euthanasia Prevention Coalition
Box 25033, London, ON, Canada N6C 6A8
(877) 439-3348
e-mail: info@epcc.ca
Web site: www.epcc.ca

The Euthanasia Prevention Coalition is a group based in Ontario, Canada, that educates and informs organizations and individuals to help them create social barriers against euthanasia and physician-assisted suicide. The group offers information packages specially tailored to each of the following audiences: schools, churches, politicians, hospice and palliative care groups, and the general public. They have also produced a DVD arguing that euthanasia and PAS are a threat to the disabled and certain vulnerable people.

Euthanasia Research and Guidance Organization (ERGO)
24829 Norris Ln., Junction City, OR 97448-9559
(541) 998-1873
e-mail: ergo@efn.org
Web site: www.finalexit.org

ERGO is a nonprofit organization founded to educate patients, physicians, and the general public about euthanasia and physician-assisted suicide. The organization serves a broad range of people: ERGO provides research for students, other "right-to-die" organizations, authors, and journalists; conducts opinion polls; drafts guidelines about how to prepare for and commit assisted suicide for physicians and patients; and counsels dying patients as long as they are competent adults in the final stages of a terminal illness.

Human Life International (HLI)
4 Family Life Ln., Front Royal, VA 22630
(800) 549-5433
fax: (540) 622-6247
e-mail: hli@hli.org
Web site: www.hli.org

HLI categorically rejects euthanasia and believes assisted suicide is morally unacceptable. It defends the rights of the unborn, the disabled, and those threatened by euthanasia, and it provides education, advocacy, and support services. HLI publishes a monthly e-newsletter, mini-newsletters on special topics, and online articles on euthanasia.

National Hospice and Palliative Care Organization
1700 Diagonal Rd., Suite 625
Alexandria, VA 22314
(703) 837-1500
e-mail: nhpco_info@nhpco.org
Web site: www.nho.org

The organization works to educate the public about the benefits of hospice care for the terminally ill and their families. It seeks to promote the idea that with the proper care and pain medication, the terminally ill can live out their lives comfortably and in the company of their families. The organization opposes euthanasia and assisted suicide.

National Right to Life Committee
512 10th St. NW, Washington, DC 20004
(202) 626-8800
e-mail: NRLC@nrlc.org
Web sie: www.nrlc.org

The committee is an activist group that opposes euthanasia and assisted suicide. NRLC publishes the monthly *NRL News* and several articles from an anti-euthanasia perspective, including the four-part position paper "Why We Shouldn't Legalize Assisting Suicide."

Not Dead Yet
7521 Madison St.
Forest Park, IL 60130
(708) 209-1500
e-mail: ndycoleman@aol.com
Web site: www.notdeadyet.org

Founded to voice the objections of disabled people against "medically assisted killing," this organization offers many archived articles, fact sheets, humor pieces, and links from an anti-euthanasia perspective.

For Further Reading

Books

Dowbiggin, Ian, *Merciful End: The Euthanasia Movement in Modern America*. New York: Oxford University Press, 2003. A Canadian professor of history gives an account of the development of the euthanasia movement in America.

Dworkin, Gerald, R.G. Frey, and Sissela Bok, *Euthanasia and Physician-Assisted Suicide: For and Against*. New York: Cambridge University Press, 1998. The authors take opposing sides to illustrate key arguments in the debate over euthanasia and physician-assisted suicide.

Foley, Kathleen M., and Herbert Hendin, eds., *The Case Against Assisted Suicide: For the Right to End-of-Life Care*. Baltimore: Johns Hopkins University Press, 2002. A collection of essays from writers in various disciplines who all argue against physician-assisted suicide.

Gorsuch, Neil M., *The Future of Assisted Suicide and Euthanasia*. Princeton, NJ: Princeton University Press, 2006. Examines the most common arguments for legalizing euthanasia and assisted dying, and then argues against legalization.

Hillyard, Daniel, and John Dombrink, *Dying Right: The Death with Dignity Movement*. New York: Routledge, 2001. An account of the successful campaign to legalize physician-assisted suicide in Oregon.

Jonsen, Albert R., *Bioethics Beyond the Headlines: Who Lives? Who Dies? Who Decides?* Lanham, MD: Rowman & Littlefield, 2005. An introduction to bioethics written for the average reader, this book addresses some of the key questions about euthanasia, among other important subjects.

Lavi, Shai J., *The Modern Art of Dying: A History of Euthanasia in the United States*. Princeton, NJ: Princeton University Press, 2005. Follows the history of euthanasia in the United States, concentrating on how people's attitudes toward death have changed over time.

Manning, Michael, *Euthanasia and Physician-Assisted Suicide: Killing or Caring?* Mahwah, NJ: Paulist Press, 1998. A physician and Roman

Catholic priest takes a stand against euthanasia and physician-assisted suicide.

Nicol, Neal, and Harry Wylie, *Between the Dying and the Dead: Dr. Jack Kevorkian's Life and the Battle to Legalize Euthanasia.* Madison: University of Wisconsin Press, 2006. An authorized biography of Dr. Jack Kevorkian, who is currently in prison for illegally assisting in the suicides of various patients.

Peck, M. Scott, *Denial of the Soul: Spiritual and Medical Perspectives on Euthanasia.* New York: Random House, 1997. A spiritual perspective on euthanasia that defines both emotional and physical suffering. Suggests guidelines for how to approach the problem of physician-assisted suicide.

Pool, Robert, *Negotiating a Good Death: Euthanasia in the Netherlands.* Binghamton, NY: Haworth, 2000. Describes euthanasia as it is practiced in the Netherlands.

President's Council on Bioethics, *Taking Care: Ethical Caregiving in Our Aging Society.* Washington, DC: Government Printing Office, 2006. Available for free at www.bioethics.gov, this book argues against euthanasia for handicapped or terminally ill people.

Quill, Timothy E., *Physician-Assisted Dying: The Case for Palliative Care and Patient Choice.* Baltimore: Johns Hopkins University Press, 2004. A collection of essays from writers in various disciplines who all advocate physician-assisted suicide.

Quinlan, Julia Duane, *My Joy, My Sorrow: Karen Ann's Mother Remembers.* Cincinnati, OH: Saint Anthony Messenger, 2005. An account of the landmark euthanasia case of Karen Ann Quinlan from the perspective of the patient's mother.

Smith, Wesley J., *Forced Exit: The Slippery Slope from Assisted Suicide to Legalized Murder.* New York: Random House, 1997. Argues against accepting euthanasia because such acceptance may well lead to a legal acceptance of the right to kill.

Periodicals

Asch, Adrienne, "Recognizing Death While Affirming Life: Can End of Life Reform Uphold a Disabled Person's Interest in Continued Life?" *Hastings Center Report,* November/December 2005.

Boyd, Andrew D., "Physician-Assisted Suicide: For and Against," American Medical Student Association, November 14, 2005.

Brennan, Phil, "Killing Schiavo Threatens Religious Freedom in U.S.," NewsMax.com, February 23, 2005.

CBC News Viewpoint, "The 'Dying with Dignity' Debate," October 26, 2005. www.cbc.ca.

Colby, Bill, "Five Minutes That Can Spare a Family Years of Pain," *USA Today*, March 7, 2005.

Coleman, Gerald D., "Take and Eat: Morality and Medically Assisted Feeding," *America*, April 5, 2004.

Craven, Nick, "When Doctors Should Be Allowed to Kill a Patient," *Daily Mail*, June 8, 2006.

Cronn, Tad, "Down a Slippery Slope: Oregon Euthanasia Law Proving to Be Unmonitorable," *Los Angeles Daily News*, April 8, 2005.

Dobrer, Jonathan, "Lives in the Balance: Times, and Attitudes Toward Euthanasia, Have Changed," *Los Angeles Daily News*, February 17, 2005.

Flynn, Tom, "The Final Freedom: Suicide and the 'New Prohibitionists,'" *Free Inquiry*, Spring 2003.

Fritz, Mark, "How Simple Device Set Off a Fight Over Elderly Care," *Wall Street Journal*, eastern edition, December 8, 2005.

Gilmore, Jodie, "Court-Ordered Euthanasia: Euthanasia Advocates Claim It Is Not a Crime to Kill as Long as the Victims Cannot Speak for Themselves," *New American*, April 4, 2005.

Golden, Marilyn, "Why Progressives Should Oppose the Legalization of Assisted Suicide," *BeyondChron: San Francisco's Alternative Online Daily News*, April 12, 2005.

Grossman, Cathy Lynn, "When Life's Flame Goes Out," *USA Today*, October 5, 2005.

Heimburger, Douglas C., "Physician-Assisted Death Should Remain Illegal: A Debate," *Journal of Biblical Ethics in Medicine*, no. 3, 1994.

Hentoff, Nat, "'Judicial Murder' and Terri Schiavo: The American Way of Euthanasia," *Washington Times*, July 11, 2005.

Horsburgh, Susan, Dietlind Lerner, and Bryce Corbett, "Her Son's Last Wish," *People*, October 13, 2003.

Hull, Richard T., "The Case for: Physician-Assisted Suicide," *Free Inquiry*, Spring 2003.

Jacoby, Susan, "The Right to Die," *AARP Bulletin*, November 2005.

Keizer, Garret, "Life Everlasting: The Religious Right and the Right to Die," *Harper's Magazine*, February 2005.

Kornblut, Ann E., "A Next Step: Making Rules to Die By," *New York Times*, April 1, 2005.

Lee, Daniel E., "Physician-Assisted Suicide: A Conservative Critique of Intervention," *Hastings Center Report*, January/February 2003.

New York Times, "The Assisted-Suicide Decision," January 19, 2006.

Palm Beach Post, "Dutch Doctors Want to Play God," November 4, 2005.

Pearce, Stephen S., "Assisted Suicide Provides Dignity, Respect for Terminally Ill," *Jewish News Weekly*, February 27, 2006.

Pew Research Center for People and the Press, "Strong Public Support for Right to Die," January 5, 2006. http://people_press.org/reports/display.php3?ReportID=266.

Ponnuru, Ramesh, "Reasons to Live: The Rational Case Against Euthanasia," *National Review*, April 25, 2005.

Quindlen, Anna, "The Culture of Each Life," *Newsweek*, April 4, 2005.

Rogatz, Peter, "The Positive Virtues of Physician-Assisted Suicide," *Humanist*, November/December 2001.

Rudden, Lawrence, and Gerard V. Bradley, "Death and the Law—Why the Government Has Interest in Preserving Life," *World and I*, May 2003.

Shibler, Ann V., "Defying the Death Culture," *New American*, May 16, 2005.

Singer, Peter, "Making Our Own Decisions About Death: Competency Should Be Paramount," *Free Inquiry*, August/September 2005.

Somerville, Margaret, "Life and Death Issues Take Centre Stage: Why, After We Have Prohibited Euthanasia for Thousands of Years, Are We Now Considering Such a Radically Different Response to Human Dying and Death?" *Montreal Gazette*, October 17, 2004.

Taylor, Stuart, Jr., "What Terri Schiavo's Case Should Teach Us," *National Journal*, April 2, 2005.

Tolson, Jay, "Wrestling with the Final Call: Ethical and Legal Issues on 'Persistent Vegetative State' and Euthanasia," *U.S. News & World Report*, April 4, 2005.

Weijer, Charles, "A Death in the Family: Reflections on the Terri Schiavo Case," *Canadian Medical Association Journal*, April 26, 2005.

Williams, Patricia J., "Habeas Corpus: Diary of a Mad Law Professor: Analyzing Implications of the Terri Schiavo Case," *Nation*, April 11, 2005.

Web Sites

Compassion & Choices (www.compassionandchoices.org). The oldest and largest organization in the United States founded to campaign for choices in dying, Compassion and Choices offers a Web site that emphasizes pain management, improving end-of-life care, and campaigning for legally-assisted suicide. The site includes many articles on pain management, care for medical conditions, and resources to learn about physician-assisted suicide.

The Death with Dignity National Center (www.dwd.org). This Web site—which is maintained by a nonpartisan, nonprofit group that has campaigned in defense of Oregon's Death with Dignity Law for over a decade—offers a bounty of articles, editorials, and news updates from a pro-euthanasia perspective.

International Task Force on Euthanasia and Assisted Suicide (www.internationaltaskforce.org and www.euthanasia.com). Founded to combat efforts to legalize euthanasia and physician-assisted suicide, this organization's main site offers links to news updates about efforts to legalize assisted suicide, as well as various articles about euthanasia and pain management. The second site offers an exhaustive archive of research materials about euthanasia, mostly from an anti-euthanasia perspective.

The Nightingale Alliance (www.nightingalealliance.org/index.php). An organization founded to combat the legalization of euthanasia and physician-assisted suicide, the Nightingale Alliance offers brochures and numerous links to news articles, pain management information, personal stories, research papers, arguments against euthanasia, and more.

Not Dead Yet (www.notdeadyet.org). Founded to voice the objections of disabled people against "medically assisted killing," this organization offers many archived articles, fact sheets, humor pieces, and links from an anti-euthanasia perspective.

The World Federation of Right to Die Societies (www.worldrtd.net). A collective of thirty-eight organizations in twenty-three countries all fighting to legalize euthanasia and physician-assisted suicide, this organization offers plentiful resources, newsletters, and articles to help people do the same.

Index

Picture Credits

Cover: Michael Crabtree/Reuters/Landov

AP/Wide World Photos, 19, 20, 35, 48

© Bruce Burkhardt/CORBIS, 99

© Dan Chung/Reuters/Landov, 70

© David Kadlubowski/CORBIS, 38

© Ed Kashi/CORBIS, 96

© Edward Kudryavitsky/CORBIS, 43

© Etienne Ansotte/epa/CORBIS, 60

© Gaetan Bally/epa/CORBIS, 67

© Gerhard V. Roon/Hollandse Hoogte/CORBIS SYGMA, 46

Getty Images, 10, 25, 29, 42, 55, 62, 85, 94, 101, 102

© Jay Maillin/Bloomberg News/Landov, 13

© Micah Walter/CORBIS, 32

© Michael Crabtree/Reuters/Landov, 65

© Newhouse News Service, 89

© Patrick Seeger/dpa/Landov, 82

Photos.com, 75, 80

© Reuters/CORBIS, 49, 93

© Reuters/Greg White/Landov, 15

© Shaun Heasley/Reuters/CORBIS, 12

© The Art Archive/CORBIS, 41

Victor Habbick Visions, 23, 36, 53, 69, 76, 87

About the Editor

Paul Cockeram teaches English at Harrisburg Area Community College in Harrisburg, Pennsylvania. He also edits manuals, articles, and books on a freelance basis. This is his first publication with Greenhaven Press.